The Complete Book of Tatting

A tatted chatelaine. In olden times ladies kept their sewing needs on little chains clipped to their waists so that they were always handy when required. Here, on tatted chains, we have a tiny hook, folding scissors, a little bag to hold your shuttle and a stitch unpicker in its tatted case.

The Complete Book of

TATTING

REBECCA JONES

Illustrations by Dean Pomfrett and the author

Dryad Press Limited   London

Dedicated to
LLOYD FENTON JONES
who put up with the rushed
meals and bits of cotton
everywhere without complaining

First published in Great Britain in 1985 by Dryad Press
First published in Australia in 1985 by Kangaroo Press

Printed in Singapore for the publishers
Dryad Press Ltd
4 Fitzhardinge Street London W1H 0AH

ISBN 0 8521 9652 0

Contents

Preface

My main aim in writing this book was to fill in the gaps and answer the questions that puzzled me when I was learning to tat many years ago.

I saw an illustration of tatting in a book and became interested. How could I learn this, I asked myself. Not having anyone who had even heard of tatting to ask, I decided to learn from a book.

Maybe I'm not very bright or suffer from lack of concentration, but I found it very hard to follow the instructions given in the book—once I finally found a book *with* instructions!

I found that one picture of two hands, one holding a shuttle and the other holding a piece of thread, and then a page of directions followed by another picture of the completed tatting knot, was not very helpful to a beginner.

I hope to remedy this by the first book to carry *complete* directions for *six* different ways to tat. If you are not successful with one method, you still have *five* more to choose from.

Tatting is very easy, once you know how, and more importantly, it is a cheap handicraft requiring very little outlay—all you need is a shuttle and a ball of thread and away you go.

With the patterns given I have used the diagram method favoured by some European and Japanese magazines as I find this a simpler and less time-consuming way to follow a pattern than having to read through written directions. With the diagram you can *see* where the joins are made and how many stitches go where.

The patterns used are either traditional or my own original designs, and I have tried to cover as many different aspects of tatting as possible. However, you will notice that there are no patterns for doilies and only one for a collar. This is because there are numerous patterns for these in most of the other tatting books available. They are both quite easily made by combining motifs and borders, or just motifs, and I suggest that readers make their own designs.

I hope that more young people will take up tatting in the future and thus keep the craft alive. Once you have mastered it, let people know by taking your tatting with you wherever you go. Tatting is small enough to slip into your pocket, purse or car glove box, so be like the fashionable ladies of the eighteenth century and let your tatting be seen everywhere!

Rebecca Jones

Acknowledgments

I would like to thank the following people who, among many others, were extremely helpful in one way or another during the production of this book.

Dean Pomfrett, for giving up valuable time when he could have been studying, to do so many line drawings at such short notice.

Miss Santina M. Levey and Miss Alyson Morris of the Department of Textiles at the Victoria and Albert Museum, London, for information on Mlle Riego.

Mrs Betty Franks of the Australian Lace Guild and the Australian Forum for the Textile Arts, Brisbane, for lots of help in all directions.

Mrs Mary Konior of the Ring of Tatters in England for her advice on Roll Tatting.

Mr Edward A. Morin of the Jiffy Tatting Needle Company, Portland, Oregon, U.S.A., for his information on his method of Needle Tatting.

Mrs Jann Johnson of the Old Sewing Box Museum, Deloraine, Tasmania, for giving me the idea of a complete tatting book in the first place.

Symbols Used in Patterns

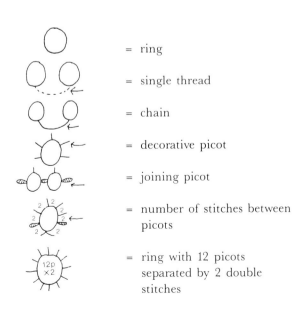

= ring

= single thread

= chain

= decorative picot

= joining picot

= number of stitches between picots

= ring with 12 picots separated by 2 double stitches

= ring with 12 picots
separated by 1 ds
(double stitch). The next
row will join on to these
picots.

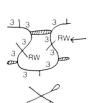

= work chain as shown
and then reverse work
and continue as directed.

= cut

= Josephine knot

= order in which work is
to be done.

Symbols Used in the Doodles Patterns

As well as the symbols used in the other patterns, there are a few extra ones used for the doodles patterns.

Instead of the short, straight line used to show picots in the other patterns, in these diagrams *only*, picots have been drawn as an oval shape to give a better idea of how the finished doodle will look.

Also, in some cases, as the picots have to be cut and sometimes frayed with a pin this had to be indicated.

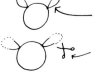

picots

picots to be cut

picots to be cut and frayed
with a pin to give a fluffy
appearance

picots which are cut at the
body and opened out to form
legs, etc.

Getting Acquainted with Tatting

What is tatting? It is, to quote Webster's dictionary 'a lace-like trimming of knotted loops and threads'. While that may be tatting in a nutshell, it does nothing to convey the delicate, exquisite, snowflake-like quality of a tatted doily, or the frothy laciness of a tatted handkerchief.

Unfortunately, there are not many examples of tatting on display in Australia and for the collector of old lace, tatted pieces are hard to come by. There does not seem to be any particular reason for this other than that perhaps families tend to keep their tatted items rather than donating them to museums or selling them to second-hand shops or antique collectors.

Also, many people have tatting in their homes and don't know it. When shown a sample of tatted lace, they say 'Oh, we have a tablecloth [doily, collar, hanky] made of that. We thought it was crocheted'. And then they show you the most exquisite piece of work that you'd give your right arm to own! One lady I know has a magnificent tablecloth made by her grandfather!

The main difference between tatting and knitting and crochet is that tatting is made from knotting threads and knitting and crochet are made by looping the thread. Tatting is made from one basic knot called a double knot (or double stitch) which is simply repeated, in either rings or chains. These knots are made over another thread, thus while looking delicate, tatting is actually quite sturdy and strong. Picots, the little loops which give the airy look to the work, are formed by simply leaving a space between the knots and then when the knots are moved along the shuttle thread this space slides up to become a loop. That's all there is to it!

It looks complicated and the directions given in many books seem hard to follow. This is usually because there are not enough step-by-step diagrams showing the way to make the stitch. However, in this book I aim to remedy this by giving complete diagrams and instructions for more than one method—including the easiest way of all which is a variation of Mlle Riego's method of 1850!

Naturally, if you have a tatting grandmother handy, it is always easier to learn from someone in person and although she may not tat in the Riego way, the end result will be the same. She will also be able to help you with the 'clicking', of the knot, often the most difficult bit to master. But more of that later.

The patterns given are all either traditional or original and tested by myself and my pupils. While you might think you'd like to just work the patterns as shown, why not experiment a bit? Try something different. Don't just use fine mercer-crochet cotton—be bold—try tatting with something like 8-ply wool instead. Just make sure the thread you use is smooth so that the knots will slide easily.

By using a thicker thread obviously you can't get as much onto the shuttle. So for thicker thread try using a plastic netting needle (available at most craft shops) as this holds quite a bit of wool or thicker thread and is easy to hold and use. Remember, a shuttle is only something to hold your thread while you tat—its size and shape doesn't really have any bearing on the finished product. Indeed, Lady Hoare (we'll be hearing about her later in the section on the history of tatting) used a shuttle which was obviously designed from an old-fashioned netting needle.

Unlike crochet or knitting, where you need different-sized hooks or needles depending on the thread used, with tatting one shuttle does for everything.

For fine work I like the Aero shuttle which has its own little hook built into it and comes with two little bobbins. Because of this in-built hook, this is a handy shuttle to take if you carry your tatting while travelling as there is no need to worry about having a crochet hook for joining.

Some people think this hook gets in the way and slows the work done, but it's all a matter of personal preference.

The Clover plastic shuttle is another one which is easy and pleasant to use. Personally, I'm not really fond of the so-called tortoiseshell shuttles (they're actually made of plastic) as they seem awkward to use as the tips are so close together, but there again, many people I know wouldn't use any other kind. (These are not to be confused with the genuine tortoiseshell shuttles which are, unfortunately, no longer made.)

You will probably end up with two or three or even more shuttles in your collection as some work calls for the use of two shuttles, so have a look around and buy the one which suits you and your needs. These are available in most big department stores either in the haberdashery or handicrafts departments, and also in many of the handicraft shops which are springing up in most suburbs these days. If you can get or borrow one of Grandma's old shuttles, do so, as there is a special feeling about using a really old shuttle.

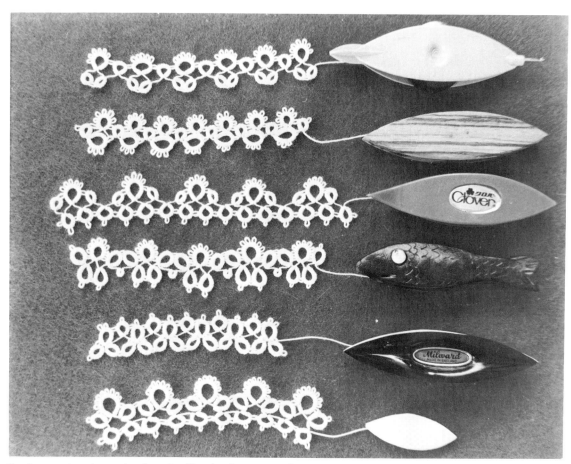

Borders made using a shuttle only. Shuttles from top to bottom are Aero, modern wooden shuttle, Clover shuttle, fish-shaped shuttle, Milward, tiny wooden shuttle.

Tatting—Origins and History

Although many sources give many derivations for the origin of the word 'tatting' no one really knows for sure. Some say because tatting is made up (or was originally) of small pieces joined together it thus resembles rags and tatters. 'Tatters' is Scandinavian in origin—from the Old Norse *taturr* and Icelandic *toturr*, both meaning rags. It has also been suggested that whilst working at their lace women *tat*tled and gossiped, but this derivation is not very likely.

In Europe it is a popular craft. The German word for tatting is *Schiffchenarbeit* meaning 'the work of the little boat' (i.e. the boat-shaped shuttle); the Italians call it *occhi* meaning 'eyes', referring to the rings which make up the lace; the Turkish say *makouk* which is their word for shuttle; the French call it *frivolité* and the Swedish word is similar—*frivolitet*—which again describes the character of the work. (South American ladies also call their tatting *frivolité*, probably from the Spanish and Portuguese connections.) The one which I find has the nicest sound to it is Finnish—*sukkulapitsi*—which combines two words which describe the whole thing—*sukkula* meaning shuttle and *pitsi* meaning lace—shuttlelace. There has even been a move in some circles to try to change the name of tatting to shuttle-lace, which, while it may be a good idea for up-dating the craft, would be very hard to put into common use.

Tatting is believed to have evolved from knotting, which in various forms is a very ancient type of decoration for clothing. The Egyptians used knotting as decoration on ceremonial dress and a mummy was found with a skirt overlay of knotted rings which look very much like tatting.

The early Chinese also used knotting and couched their knotted designs into their embroideries. These eventually found their way to Europe and knotting was popular for the decoration of furnishings and embroideries in Medieval times—Chaucer even mentions it in his *Canterbury Tales* (1387).

Knotting was worked by winding thread onto a shuttle and then making a series of knots on the thread at close intervals so that the work looked like a string of beads. However, it did not become really popular until the seventeenth century when it is thought that the Dutch, due to their trading in the East, brought new forms of knotting from China and made it commonplace in Europe.

It is not quite clear where the transition from knotting to tatting took place, but it is generally thought to have occurred in Italy. Someone sitting knotting one day decided to join her knots into a ring instead of making a string of them and thus tatting was born.

Meanwhile in England, in the court of William and Mary, knotting was in full swing. Queen Mary was herself an ardent knotter and took it everywhere with her. Indeed, there was even a poem written about her by Sir Charles Sedley in which he compares her to the former Catholic queens who were always

'. . . . . telling beads,
But here's a Queen now, thanks to God,
Who, when she rides in coach abroad
Is always knotting threads.'

Being a favourite pastime of the ladies at Court, naturally the shuttles were very elaborate and expensive, being made as much to be seen as to be used. Knotting shuttles were much larger than the present tatting shuttles, being between 13 cm and 15 cm long and 2.5 cm and 5 cm wide, with the blades open at the ends so that quite thick threads might be wound on. Some very precious threads were used for knotting including gold thread.

Ivory and tortoiseshell decorated and inlaid with gold and silver and mother-of-pearl were popular for shuttles, which were often given as gifts. In 1745, the Infanta Maria Theresa was given five caskets of enamelled gold each containing a gold shuttle as a wedding present. Madame de Pompadour also had elaborate gold shuttles, each decorated with jewels.

The French knotting shuttles were even larger than the English ones, and again, the ladies at Court used their shuttles almost as a fashion accessory. In fashionable society a lady never sat empty-handed and idle. She used either her fan or her knotting shuttle to show off her hands and to make her look composed and graceful as well as industrious.

Shuttles were carried in little knotting bags which were also richly adorned and bejewelled and these little bags were taken everywhere from society parties to the theatre. A fashionable lady would not be seen without one. Indeed, many ladies had their portrait painted complete with knotting bag and shuttle.

As mentioned previously, tatting, as such, is thought to have originated in Italy in the sixteenth century. It was probably made by nuns, as many forms of lace and needlework owe their existence to convents. The early forms of tatting were quite different from today. There were no chains and the work consisted of only rings, which were made in rows or groups using only a single shuttle and then tied or sewn together afterwards. Sometimes the rings were made with a needle instead of a shuttle.

During the early eighteenth century tatting was gradually taking over from knotting in England, although the word *tatting* did not actually appear in print until 1843. It is thought that early examples of tatting were still referred to as knotting.

A Mrs Mary Delaney in 1750 made a pair of chair covers having a border of oak leaves in white linen which were outlined in knotted

threads, some of which are tatted rather than knotted. Later, in 1781, Parson Woodforde mentions buying a pair of small ivory shuttles for his niece for one shilling. It is presumed that these shuttles were for tatting since knotting shuttles were of a much larger size.

At the start of the nineteenth century tatting was a popular English occupation and in 1843 the *Ladies Handbook of Millinery, Dressmaking and Tatting* was published. This was to be the start of many books on the subject. Up to this time tatting patterns were passed down from tatter to tatter by word of mouth or simply copying other pieces of work.

Shortly after this, in 1850, the woman regarded as the 'mother' of modern tatting appeared on the scene. She was Mademoiselle Eleonore Riego de la Branchardiere, a half-Irish, half-French woman who had a 'fancy warehouse' in London and supplied lace-making and embroidery materials.

Between 1850 and 1868 Mlle Riego (as she liked to be known) published eleven little pattern books showing mainly borders and insertions in tatting. Mlle Riego used picots to join the rings together but she used a needle to do it at first and not a shuttle, as it wasn't until 1851 that an unknown writer published instructions on how to join with a shuttle and so improved the method of tatting.

Mlle Riego also developed the use of a central

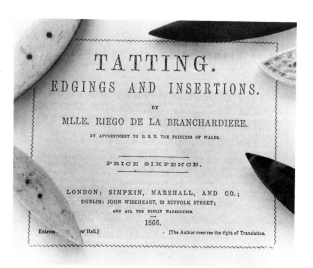

Title page of one of Mlle Riego's tatting books. These booklets were very small in size, being only about 15 cm by 12 cm and had about sixteen pages of patterns. The antique shuttles in a clockwise direction from the top right hand corner are: treen (wooden) about 1870; carved ivory, 1800; tortoiseshell, 1870; whalebone, 1860; bone, 1860.

ring with picots as the central motif and many old patterns use this as the basis of their design. If you are lucky enough to have any old piece of tatting (really old!) you will notice that it consists of 'wheels'—that is, a central small ring with about twelve picots, then a second row of small rings joined to these picots and an outer row of rings joined to the second row by a single thread. These wheels are then joined together side by side to go round a doily or whatever, or are joined together round a central 'wheel' to form a complete tatted doily.

The name doily, by the way, comes from a Mr D'Oyley who kept a small shop in The Strand in London in the eighteenth century, selling cloth and small pieces of material which were fringed or decorated and used to put under finger bowls and the like to stop them marking tables.

Because chains were not invented until 1864 Mlle Riego used to crochet over the single threads left between rings to make a firmer lace.

At about the same time that Mlle Riego was enlightening the English ladies, a Mrs Pullan

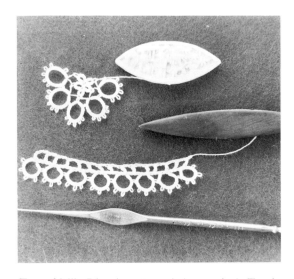

Two of Mlle Riego's patterns being worked. Top is part of the 'Florentine Border' and below is 'Scallop Edging'. This one is very interesting to modern tatters as chains were not in use at this time so the rings were made with a single thread between them and were not closed fully. Then when the required length had been made, these single threads were crocheted over to make a heading as shown in the photograph.

published a book in America with a section on tatting. This was in 1853 and in 1857 the same lady had an edging featured in a popular ladies magazine of the day.

An attempt was made in 1847 to introduce tatting as a cottage industry in Ireland at a place called Ardee, but it was not very successful. Irish tatting, while usually worked in very fine thread, did not show a great deal of originality in design, being made up mostly of repeated motifs worked into collars and cuffs.

Mrs Beeton (of cooking fame) also wrote a *Book of Needlework* in 1870 and this included a section on tatting.

Probably the main authority on tatting after Mlle Riego was Mlle Therese de Dillmont, a French woman who wrote what is considered by many to be the needlework bible—her *Encyclopedia of Needlework* published in 1886 and still available and selling well today. In the chapter on tatting Mlle de Dillmont covers many types of edgings and braids as well as projects such as bedspreads combining tatting and crochet. She also describes how to use two shuttles and the use of two colours in the threads. Mlle de Dillmont is credited with inventing the Josephine knot, which we will discuss later.

Back in England ten years later a schoolteacher, Mrs Louisa Walker, wrote a little book called *Varied Occupations in String Work* which consisted of fairly simple exercises for young children to make by knotting string in macramestyle patterns. However, in one section she deals with single and double tatted bars which are worked with one string upon a foundation string. Naturally, the knot is worked by hand and not with a shuttle. Mrs Walker also explains how to make loop fringes (picots) and single and double loop rosettes (rings). One very interesting exercise is joining the double looped fringes (which are very similar to Riego's Pearl Tatting) together by interlocking the loops in much the same way that hairpin crochet strips are joined together (fig. 1).

The next major advance in tatting was in 1910 when Lady Katherine Hoare wrote *The Art of Tatting* and used her own work and that of Queen Marie of Romania as examples. Queen Marie

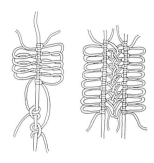

Fig. 1   Mrs Walker's looped fringes

made many creative articles, often for the church, using gold threads and jewels worked into the pieces. Lady Hoare popularised the use of the chain and wrote: 'with two shuttles and an imaginative brain there is no end to the designs that may be invented' (fig. 2).

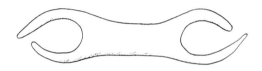

Fig. 2.   Lady Hoare's wooden shuttle

Tatting was reasonably popular during the 1920s and 1930s but then it went into a decline. In America it has remained fairly common all along, with many magazines and various thread companies printing patterns quite often. One of the leading American designers is Myrtle Hamilton who turns out an amazing number of designs of all kinds on a regular basis.

In Australia, during the 1930s and 1940s tatting enjoyed quite a revival, with many original Australian patterns available to keen tatters. One of the leading designers was Norma Benporath who for many years kept everyone's shuttle busy with her lovely patterns in *Australian Home Beautiful*. The most amazing thing about Miss Benporath's prolific output was that every article used in the illustrations to her patterns was made by Norma herself and the embroidery was done by her mother.

The old *Australian Woman's Mirror* often featured very attractive little patterns by Rachel Abraham during the 1940s.

In my search for information on old patterns I have several times come across pages torn from these magazines and carefully saved in scrapbooks of patterns. Some could hardly be read, they are so worn and fragile, but all were eagerly shown to me as treasures (which they are), usually by older ladies who now, sadly, no longer tat.

After the war interest in tatting waned, as with many crafts. During the 1960s and 1970s the most notable books on tatting were the rather basic but easy-to-follow book by Bessie Attenborough which reprinted many of the J. & P. Coats designs (from their various pattern books), three books by Elgiva Nicholls which treat tatting in a very contemporary, free-style manner totally unlike any of the traditional methods seen previously, and another similar book by an American writer Rhoda Auld, which, while having some very modern ideas about tatting, also gives a good history of the art plus many illustrations. The other book worth reading is by Irene Waller, again with many illustrations describing the various forms tatting can take.

With the trend towards being 'crafty' these days, tatting is one of the 'new' old crafts being rediscovered, and with this book I hope that many younger people will realise that tatting does not just have to be doilies and hankies—there is a whole world of imagination waiting to be explored.

A Word about Threads

The main requirement in a thread for tatting is that it is tightly twisted and highly mercerised. That is to say, it must be very smooth and firm. I use only Coats Mercer-Crochet cotton as I find it to be the most suitable of the many threads at present on the market.

The word mercerise means to treat the thread with a caustic alkali so as to impart a high sheen resembling that of silk, and it is this process which makes it possible for the tatted knot to slide easily along the shuttle thread.

Some of the other threads on the market, which we cannot mention by name (but you will know them if you have tried them!), do not have this smooth silky finish, and because of this, start to unravel and acquire a fuzzy look long before you have finished your piece of tatting. Some threads which are quite suitable for crocheting are not very good for tatting.

With crochet cottons the higher the size number, the finer the thread. Thus a 100 cotton is very fine and a size 20 or 10 is much thicker. For tatting around hankies most people use a 60 or even an 80 thread. If you're really confident use 100, but even a 40 makes a nice edging and it has the advantage of being available in quite a choice of colours for those who wish to make a coloured border.

If you want to tat with wool, make sure it is a smooth-textured thread. Don't try with one of the fluffy or fancy types as the knots won't slide. If you're a bit doubtful, make a slip knot in a loose end of the ball of wool and just see if it slides easily up and down when you push it. If it does slide, the wool is probably suitable.

There is one thing to remember about tatting with wool and that is that the wool will lose its softness once it is tatted. Unlike a knitted or crocheted woollen article which retains body and softness when finished, a tatted item is quite hard and firm with no 'give' to it. It still has the warmth if you make a shawl from motifs, for instance, but it just lacks something compared to a knitted or crocheted one.

Nylon ribbon, the kind used to cover coat-hangers and make shopping bags, can be tatted quite successfully as long as you make sure it is fully stretched as you wind your shuttle and make your knots. It works up into a very firm finish and is ideal for hard-wearing placemats and such.

Experiment with any odd threads you can find. The only thing you have to remember is that they must have a smooth finish so that the knots may slide easily.

Before We Start Tatting

It is a good idea to have a small bag or box to keep all your tatting things together. Apart from various shuttles (you're bound to want more than one) and various threads you will probably find some or all of the following articles will be useful.

1. A small crochet hook for joining picots. Some shuttles have a built-in hook for this purpose. The Milward shuttle has a separate little hook with it when you buy it, but as these are easily lost it's a good idea to tie a ribbon or thread to it and then either pin it to yourself or hang it round your neck.

Victorian ladies used a small ring to which a small hook or pin was attached by means of a chain. The ring was then worn over the left thumb and the hook could be picked up by the right hand when needed. These pins were also used for making picots, which were called purls in those days and worked in a slightly different fashion.

2. A stitch unpicker—the type used for unpicking hems etc. This is really a vital piece of equipment as sooner or later even the best tatter will have to unpick some stitches. One of the drawbacks to tatting is that if you make a

Things to have in your tatting bag. The bag itself, (top right), shuttles, threads, note pad and pencil, small mirror, plastic discs from sliced bread packets, modern-day chatelaine made from a large safety pin with (on chains from old bracelets) small hook, scissors, fine needle in magnifying glass handle, unpicker. The safety pin is pinned to the tatter and everything is handy for when it is required.

mistake, unlike knitting or crochet, you cannot just pull a thread and it comes undone. Unfortunately, it has to be unpicked, half stitch by half stitch

Usually the best idea is to cut the mistake off, make a join and start again. However, this is not always possible, so have your unpicker handy.

3. A pair of sharp scissors. You will need to cut ends of threads very close to your work and sharp scissors are best. Small folding ones are extra handy to keep in the little bag with your tatting things.

4. A small mirror—preferably without any edge or frame. Whatever for? you ask. This will prove to be most necessary. In many pattern books when an edging or border is shown, only a straight piece of tatting is illustrated—no corner. How do you go round the corner with no picture or instructions? You put your mirror on the

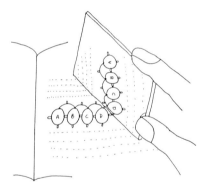

Fig. 3.   Working a corner with the aid of a mirror

picture of the straight lace at such an angle that when you look in your mirror you have formed a right angle in the lace border. This will show you if you need to make more pattern repeats to go round the corner easily and without stretching and pulling (fig. 3).

5. Thread-winders. No Victorian lady's workbox was complete without several little mother-of-pearl thread-winders. These were usually like stars or crosses and held all the left-over ends of thread. While mother-of-pearl is a bit harder to come by these days, we have something which serves just as well and is free. The little plastic discs which close the packets of sliced bread are ideal for keeping odds and ends of thread tidy.

6. A fine needle (and possibly a needle threader) for sewing in the ends of thread when you have finished a piece of tatting. Some people tie their ends in a square knot and then cut them but for a really neat finish it is better to sew them in. Details on how to do this are given later. Of course, if you are using a thicker thread, you will need an assortment of needles.

7. A small notepad and pencil for jotting down any patterns you may come across or ideas for new projects.

You will probably think of other things you need once you start tatting, but these are just a few suggestions which may help you get started. A small bag such as the ones sold in department stores as make-up or toiletry bags is ideal to hold everything you may need.

How to Tat

Winding the Shuttle

If the shuttle has a hook on the end, have the hook at the top and facing to the left. Shuttles with just a tapered point should have the point at the top and closest to you (fig. 4).

It is not absolutely necessary to tie your thread

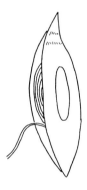

Fig. 4.   A correctly wound shuttle

through the little hole which is often in the support between the two blades—you can just thread it through and hold it in place as you start winding. The thread should be wound firmly, but not too tightly, in a clockwise direction around the shuttle, taking it between the blades to wind around the support.

Do not take the thread beyond the blades as it will not only get grubby while you are tatting, but it could also force the blades apart at the points and this will cause the thread to unwind if your shuttle is hanging loose.

For most of the methods of tatting shown in this book the thread should come from the bottom left-hand side of the shuttle. If tatting the traditional way (method two) the thread should come from the right of the shuttle.

If you are making a pattern using just rings, cut the thread from the ball before starting work. If making chains, leave the ball attached to the shuttle.

Method One—The Reverse Riego Method

The reason I call this the Reverse Riego Method is because when Mlle Riego published her instructions on how to tat in 1850 she used the same method, only she did it the other way around. (See the chapter on Mlle Riego for her full instructions.)

Riego's description of the single stitch (we call it the first half of the double stitch) is the same as our second half of the stitch and her second half is the same as our first half.

Directions all the way through are given for right-handed tatters, but in my experience, left-handed people have no difficulty in following them as both hands are used about equally—possibly the left hand a little more than the right. Should you have trouble though, hold a mirror to the diagrams. Only the left hand has been drawn as the right hand does little more than carry the shuttle.

How to make the double stitch

The first half

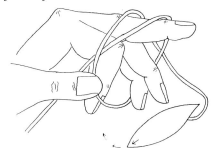

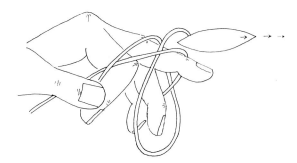

Fig. 5. After filling the shuttle and cutting the thread from the ball, wind the thread around the left hand and then pass the shuttle thread *over* the first thread.

Fig. 8. Once it has passed under the thread, the shuttle is taken to the right. Be sure to keep a firm hold on the two threads between the thumb and forefinger.

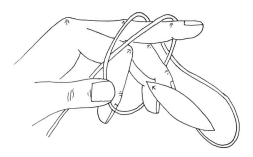

Fig. 6. Bring the shuttle round and pass it *under* the first thread and take the shuttle towards the right. Don't have too big a gap between the hands—about fifteen or twenty centimetres is plenty. If you have too long a thread you will find it awkward to handle. The more accomplished you become at tatting, the shorter the gap will get.

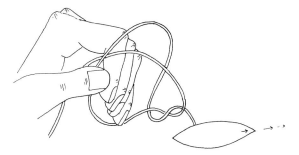

Fig. 9. Drop all the fingers and let the threads fall slightly, still taking the shuttle towards the right. As you can see, there is now a knot in the threads.

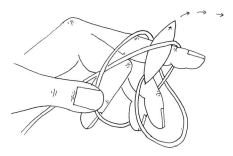

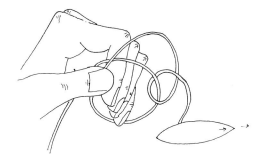

Fig. 7. The shuttle passes under the first thread. Keep the fingers spread out to form a ring.

Fig. 10. The first half of the stitch is nearly formed. However, it is still formed by the shuttle thread instead of the ring thread (the thread around the hand). This is where beginners find the main difficulty in forming the knot, but by following the instructions carefully, it's not hard to do.

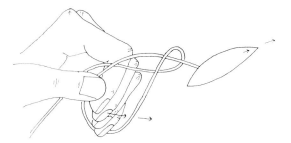

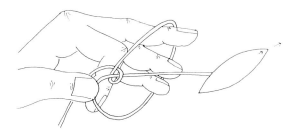

Fig. 11. Pull the shuttle thread firmly towards the right whilst raising the middle finger of the left hand. This will cause the knot to 'click' over from the shuttle thread to the ring thread. You will feel a definite 'click' as it changes position.

The knot will only change from one thread to the other if the ring thread around the hand is allowed to slacken slightly and the shuttle thread is kept taut.

Fig. 13. The first half of the stitch is now in place and you are ready to start the second half.

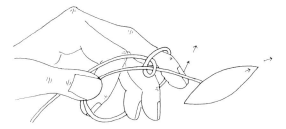

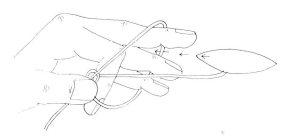

Fig. 12. The knot is now on the correct thread, so keeping the left hand spread out to keep the ring in shape, gently slide the knot you have just made along the shuttle thread towards the thumb and forefinger. With practice, you will find it easy to slip the first half into place near the thumb and forefinger by just raising the middle finger slowly and at the same time pulling on the shuttle thread.

Don't under any circumstances pull the shuttle thread towards you as this will very often cause the knot to turn back onto the other thread. By having a fairly short space between the shuttle and the left hand it is easier to push the stitch into place. If you find that you do tend to pull the shuttle thread towards yourself, try 'walking' your fingers along the shuttle thread, keeping it taut all the time, until you can reach the half stitch and can then push it into place with your finger, ensuring it has no chance of turning on itself.

Fig. 14. Keeping the ring taut and holding the first half of the stitch between the thumb and forefinger, raise the middle finger and pass the shuttle thread *under* the back loop of the ring and *over* the top loop.

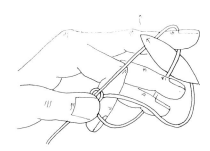

Fig. 15. The shuttle actually passes through the space formed between the middle and ring fingers of the left hand. Take the shuttle through and towards the right.

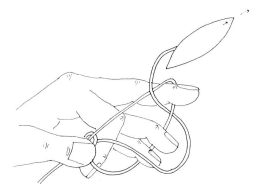

Fig. 16. The movement of the shuttle is quite clearly shown here. As mentioned before, be careful not to pull the shuttle towards yourself.

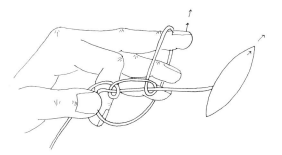

Fig. 19. Now the second half of the double stitch can be moved along the shuttle thread by raising the middle finger slowly. If you've done it correctly, and it looks like the diagram, it will slide into place next to the first half.

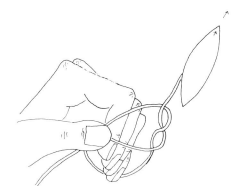

Fig. 17. Drop the fingers slowly and you will see the second half of the knot starting to form.

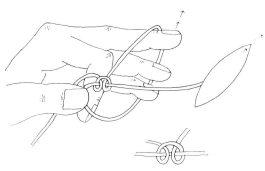

Fig. 20. The finished double stitch. To make the next double stitch, hold the completed stitch between thumb and forefinger and repeat the whole procedure, making sure that the first half of the new stitch is placed close to the previous stitch.

Now that you have made a double stitch, you must check to see if it will slide along the shuttle thread, as this is necessary to enable the rings to be closed. Just hold the stitch between the thumb and forefinger and slide it up and down the shuttle thread. If it moves freely, you have made your stitch properly and can now make some more. If it doesn't slide, it's back to square one (or should I say fig. 5) and study the diagrams more closely.

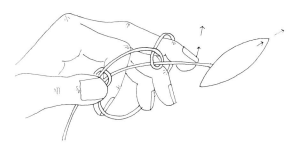

Fig. 18. Keeping the shuttle thread taut and to the right, raise the middle finger slowly, but this time on the other side of the knot. The knot is now between the middle finger and the forefinger.

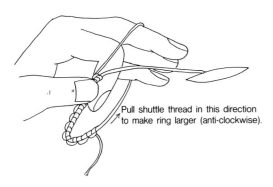

Pull shuttle thread in this direction to make ring larger (anti-clockwise).

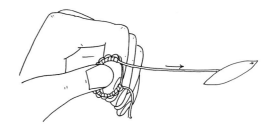

Fig. 22

Fig. 21. As the work progresses the ring of thread will get smaller as the thread around the hand is used to make the stitches. To make the ring larger, pull the shuttle thread in an anti-clockwise direction from the point where the stitches started, holding the stitches firmly whilst doing so.

Fig. 22. When you have made several stitches successfully, the ring may be closed in the following manner. Hold the double stitches gently but firmly between the thumb and forefinger and pull the shuttle thread in a clockwise direction. This will gather the knots together and they will form a tight ring as the shuttle thread is pulled.

Unfortunately, stitches made over the wrong thread look very similar to correctly made stitches and will also slide along, but on the ring thread not the shuttle thread, so be sure that your stitches slide on the shuttle thread.

Method Two—The Traditional Method

This is the method of tatting used by the majority of modern tatters, so although I have called it the traditional method it is also the modern way. It is hard to establish just when and where it actually evolved, but it has been around since just before the turn of the century and probably came from Europe—possibly France. When using this method of tatting, the thread comes from the right side of the shuttle, not the left as in the previous method.

The main thing to remember is that whichever method you choose to tat, the end result is (or should be) the same. The stitch must be formed by the thread which lies over the back of your hand and it must slide freely along the shuttle thread.

You may even invent your own method by combining a bit of one way and a bit of another, but however you do it, find the way most comfortable to you, don't worry about the way

someone else is tatting. Also, the method of making chains with the ball thread or working with two shuttles is the same regardless of which way you actually make the stitch. That is to say, you still pass the ball thread across the back of the hand and anchor it around the little finger.

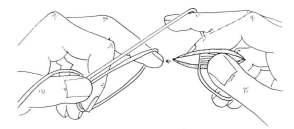

Fig. 23. One of the main differences with this method is that the shuttle is held in a horizontal position rather than vertical as in the previous method. The thread is wound around the left hand as before but then it is taken over the

middle finger of the right hand and around the other fingers of the right hand for tension, keeping the shuttle thread taut. The shuttle is held horizontally between the thumb and forefinger of the right hand.

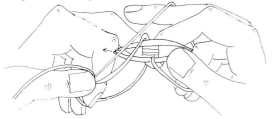

Fig. 24. The shuttle is passed *under* both threads by sliding the shuttle close to the thread around the left hand without actually lifting the right forefinger which is holding the shuttle, keeping the middle finger of the right up, with the shuttle thread taut all the time.

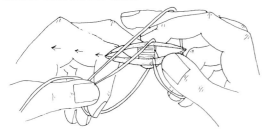

Fig. 25. This shows the right forefinger sliding over the ring thread as the shuttle slides under it.

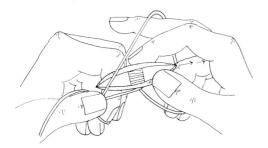

Fig. 26. Once the shuttle has passed completely under the ring thread around the left hand, slide it back towards the right in the same manner, that is, keeping it very close to the ring thread so that the thumb, this time, does not actually leave the shuttle—the thread is slipped between thumb and the shuttle. The shuttle faces in the same direction for the whole manoeuver—the point or front of the shuttle always faces to the left.

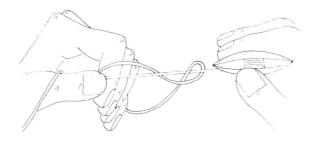

Fig. 27. The fingers of the left hand are dropped so that the ring thread becomes slack and the shuttle thread is held taut. This causes the knot to be formed by the ring thread over the shuttle thread.

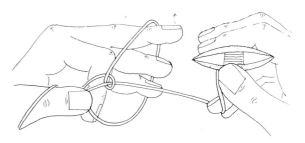

Fig. 28. The middle finger of the left hand is raised causing the first half of the stitch to slide down to the thumb and forefinger where it is held while the second half is being made.

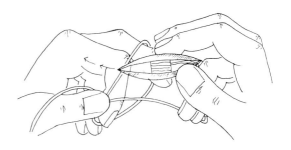

Fig. 29. The shuttle thread coming from the first half of the stitch to the shuttle is held taut by looping it around the little finger of the right hand and then the shuttle is passed *over* the ring thread round the left hand in the same manner as before, with the thread just sliding between the thumb and the shuttle without taking them apart.

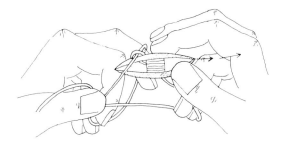

Fig. 30. When the full length of the shuttle has passed over the thread it is taken backwards towards the right with the thread sliding between the shuttle and the right forefinger this time.

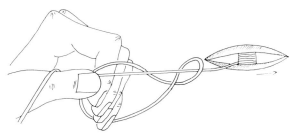

Fig. 31. Again, the fingers of the left hand are

dropped so that the ring thread becomes slack and again the shuttle is taken (backwards) to the right and held taut so that the second half of the stitch may form properly.

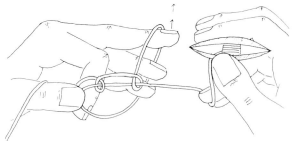

Fig. 32. The middle finger of the left hand is raised and the second half of the double stitch slides down to join the first. The whole thing is then repeated for the required number of times. The stitch must be able to slide along the shuttle thread in all methods of tatting.

Method Three—The Loop Method

I call this the loop method because you make a loop and just pass the shuttle through it to make each half of the stitch. It's basically the same as the reverse Riego method but you might find it a bit simpler to understand.

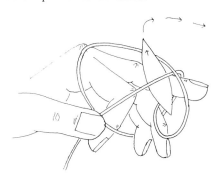

Fig. 33. The thread is passed round the left hand to form the ring thread. The thread from

the shuttle is then looped over the top of the left hand and over the ring thread too. The shuttle is passed *under* the ring thread and into the loop. It is taken through the loop and away to the right.

For the next stages refer to figs 9–13 of the Reverse Riego method of making the first half of the double stitch.

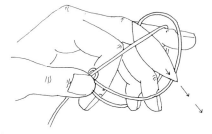

Fig. 34. For the second half of the stitch a loop is formed coming from the thumb and forefinger

of the left hand, hanging loosely down towards you. Take the shuttle round towards the middle finger of the left hand and pass the shuttle *under* the ring thread into the hanging loop and away towards the right. Now follow the rest of the second half of the double stitch of the Reverse Riego method (figs 17–20).

Method Four—The Direct Method

I call this the direct method because the thread is actually twisted into position and the shuttle is passed through the already looped and twisted thread. There are no complicated hand movements or 'clickings' to contend with. It is based on needle tatting, which is explained later. The main difference in appearance while working this method is that sometimes when you begin you seem to be making the stitches form upside down, but they will soon right themselves. It is a good method for would-be tatters who cannot master the other methods for some reason or other and also for those who may have problems with their hands such as rheumatism or arthritis.

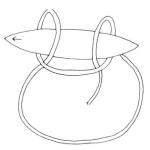

Fig. 35. This method may be worked by either holding the thread and shuttle in the hands or laying them on the table or even your lap and arranging them as shown in the diagrams.

Lay the thread as shown and pass the shuttle through the loops in the manner shown.

Fig. 37. To make the first half of the next stitch pass the thread coming from the last stitch over the shuttle in the same way as shown in the diagram. Now slide this ready-made first half along the shuttle and close up to the previous stitch.

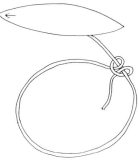

Fig. 36. Pass the two loops on to the shuttle thread and gently pull the loops tight (not too tight!) until they make a knot like the double knot.

Fig. 38. Make the second half of the stitch as shown and slide it along to the first half. Make as many stitches as required and close the ring in the same way as for normal tatting, by holding the double stitches and gently pulling the shuttle thread.

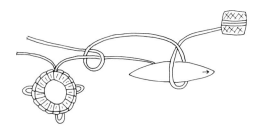

Fig. 39a

Fig. 39. Chains may also be made using this method of tatting. Again, you may either hold the work or lay it on the table.

After working the ring, reverse the work as usual and lay a thread from the ball of thread alongside the ring. Now make the loop as before (with the ball thread) and pass the shuttle through it and proceed as you did for the ring. When you have made sufficient stitches for the chain, reverse the work again and continue with another ring, and so on.

If using a ball thread still connected to the shuttle, use it in the same way—see fig. 39a.

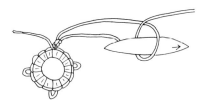

Fig. 40. This shows the first half of the second stitch of the chain being made. Picots may be made by leaving a gap between stitches.

Method Five—Wrong-way Tatting

Although this method of tatting goes against all the rules and would make traditionalists shudder with horror, it does, nevertheless, produce a form of tatting which looks very similar to the real thing and might be the answer to those would-be tatters who just *cannot* get the thread to flick over properly.

The reason I call it wrong-way tatting is that the knots are made with the *shuttle* thread over the thread which goes around the hand—in other words, the complete opposite of all the other methods of tatting.

If you are a competent tatter you may find some difficulty working this method at first, as your normal reaction is to pull the shuttle thread taut to enable the ring thread to flick over and make the knot. However, the thread around the hand must be kept taut at all times and the shuttle thread makes the knot.

The ball thread and the shuttle thread are both used at all times.

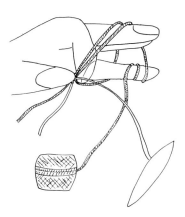

Fig. 41. Wind the ball thread around the left hand, holding the end between the thumb and forefinger and then catching it again after passing it round the hand to form a ring as you would if making a normal ring. However, now

pass the thread over the back of the fingers again as far as the little finger and then wind it round the little finger several times to anchor it.

This means you now have a ring around the left hand with a double thread across the back of the hand. Hold the loose end of the shuttle thread between the thumb and forefinger also.

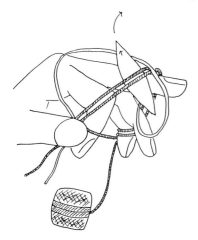

Fig. 42. Make a loop on the back of the left hand and pass the shuttle *under* the double ring thread and into the loop. Take the shuttle through the loop as in normal tatting, but *instead* of taking it towards the right and pulling it taut, keep the double ring thread taut around the hand and bring the shuttle towards you.

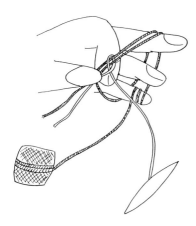

Fig. 43. This will cause the knot to be formed by the shuttle thread *over* the double thread.

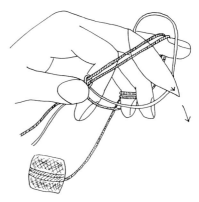

Fig. 44. Now make a loop to hang below the ring round your hand and pass the shuttle under the double thread and towards you, keeping the ring thread taut.

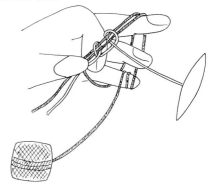

Fig. 45. This has formed the second half of the double stitch and you will notice that it appears to be upside down, but don't worry about that at the moment.

Fig. 46. Continue making the required number of double stitches, including picots (just leave a space as usual).

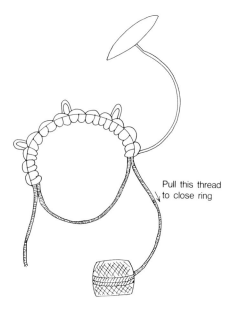

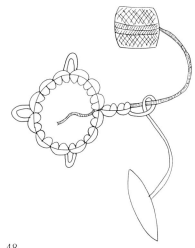

Fig. 48

Fig. 47. When all the stitches are made, slip the ring off the hand and turn it up the right way— that is, so that the picots are at the top. Holding the stitches firmly but not too tightly, gently pull the thread which goes to the ball. This will gather up the stitches and close the ring.

Fig. 48. To make a chain, the knots are still made with the shuttle thread, this time over the single ball thread. Push the stitches up close to the previous ring before starting the next one.

Joins are made by pulling a loop of the *shuttle* thread through the picot to be joined and then passing the shuttle through this loop after making sure that the picot is in place close to the previous stitch. If the join is made with the double thread the ring will not pull closed.

The main drawback to this method of tatting is that shuttle-only patterns are virtually impossible to do neatly. They can be done but there is a double thread between each ring instead of the usual single one and it doesn't look very tidy.

Method Six—Needle Tatting

Some people say that needle tatting is not true tatting as the knot is not transferred from one thread to the other, but the end result looks like tatting made with a shuttle, so we will include it in this section on how to tat.

Mlle Riego gave instructions for needle tatting using a darning needle in the 1850s, and she used a needle to make her joins originally (see chapter on Victorian tatting).

There is also a method of needle tatting which is popular in Norway and the Scandinavian countries called *Nuperella* which uses a fifteen-

centimetre long steel wire something like a fine knitting needle with a point on one end and a crochet hook on the other.

Another kind of needle tatting fast gaining many fans is 'Jiffy Needle Tatting'. This form of tatting was invented by Edward and Selma Morin of Portland, Oregon, in the late 1970s using a needle they designed called the 'Jiffy Tatting Needle' which is something like a double-ended knitting needle with an eye at one end. This enables thicker thread such as knitting wool to be used, thus the tatting makes up

'Pull this thread to close ring'

quickly into many interesting items. The address of the Jiffy Needle Company may be found at the end of the Bibliography.

Needle tatting is very simple and can be worked in rings and chains just as with normal tatting. It is an ideal method to introduce children to tatting.

The most common method of needle tatting is to cut a length of thread from the ball and make your stitches over the needle with it. However, this limits how much you can do without a join, so I have devised a much easier method using the thread directly from the ball.

One word of advice here, which I have never seen mentioned elsewhere in writings on needle tatting. The size of the needle is important in relation to the thread being used. Use a needle whose thickness is as close as possible to the thickness of the thread you are using. That is to say, if you are needle tatting using wool you can use a darning needle, but if you are using crochet cotton find a fine needle.

The reason for this is that the stitches are made on the needle itself. Consequently, if you have a fine thread over a thick needle, when you come to slide them off the stitches will be very loose and floppy. Experiment with different-sized needles and you will see what I mean. Also, try to get a needle which does not have too much of a bump where the eye is or the stitches will not slide off easily, particularly if you have made them a bit tight. (A longer needle is better than a short one, too, as it is easier to manage.)

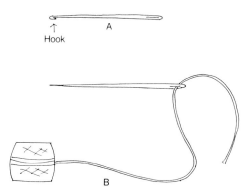

Fig. 49. If you can bend the tip of the needle into a little hook (fig. 49a) it will help when making joins. It isn't absolutely essential and the

tip often breaks off when you try to bend it, but it does help a bit.

Thread the needle from the ball of thread and pull about fifteen or twenty centimetres through the eye. This length of thread is a trial and error thing as you don't need as much as you think you do, but about fifteen centimetres will be plenty for practice (fig. 49b).

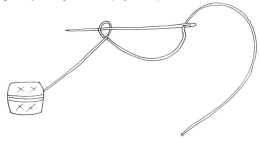

Fig. 50. Using the thread between the needle and the ball of thread, wind it around the needle as shown. This forms the first half of the double stitch.

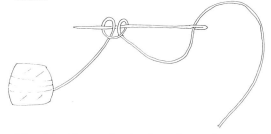

Fig. 51. Now twist the thread over the needle in the opposite direction, as shown. This makes the second half of the double stitch.

Fig. 52

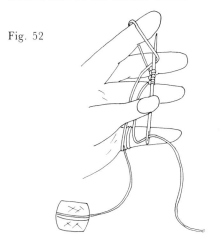

Figs 52, 53. These two diagrams show a way of

29

Fig. 53

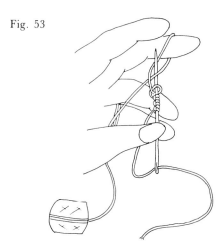

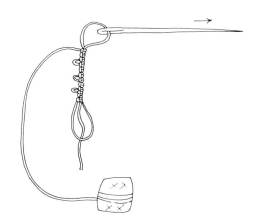

holding the needle and the thread which will speed up the work once you are used to it. The first half of the stitch is made by hooking the thread over the needle with the forefinger of the left hand and the second half is made by hooking the thread over with the middle finger.

Fig. 55. You now have the stitches sitting on a thread with the needle at one end and a loop at the other. Pull the needle carefully until the loose end is right through the stitches and there is just a small loop at the other end.

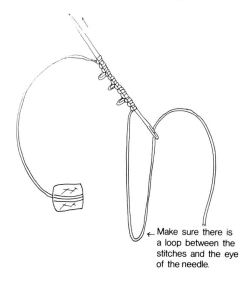

← Make sure there is a loop between the stitches and the eye of the needle.

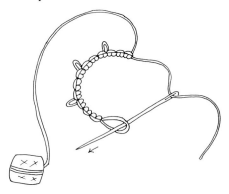

Fig. 56. To make a ring, pass the needle through the small loop and you will see that this curves the stitches round into a circle.

Fig. 54. When a sufficient number of stitches (including picots—just leave a space) have been made on the needle, slide them off to form a ring.

Make sure that there is a loop of a few centimetres between the stitches and the eye of the needle (see diagram) and then, holding the stitches gently, just pull the needle slowly through them, being sure not to pull the loop right through the stitches.

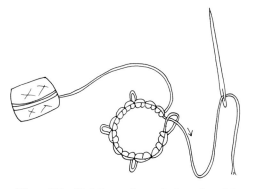

Fig. 57. Holding the stitches in this circle, carefully pull the needle so that it tightens the ring.

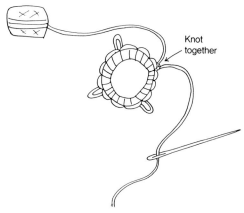

Fig. 58. When the ring has been pulled tightly closed, knot the ball thread and the needle thread tightly at the base of the ring.

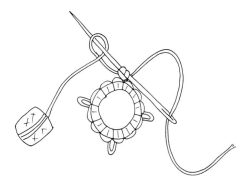

Fig. 59. You are now ready to make a chain, so hold the needle close to the base of the ring and wind the ball thread round the needle to form the first half of the double stitch. Make sure it is as close as possible to the ring.

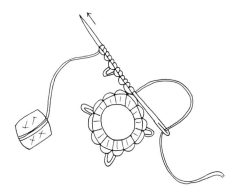

Fig. 60. Continue making the required number of stitches for the chain, keeping the stitches on

the needle until finished. Then, holding the stitches as before, pull the needle through the stitches until it is right through.

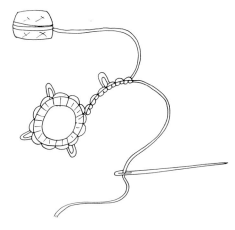

Fig. 61. There is no need to leave a loop at the other end of the stitches as this time they do not have to be pulled into a circle. Make sure that the stitches are pushed down close to the ring before starting the next ring.

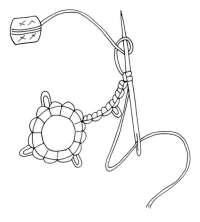

Fig. 62. Reverse the work and start the stitches as before, making the first one close to the last stitch of the chain.

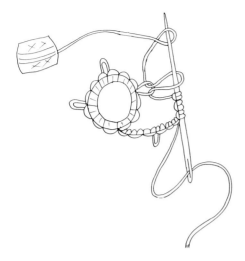

Make your stitches on needle B using the thread from needle A as shown in the diagram.

When the required number of stitches have been made pass needle B through the stitches taking both threads right through the stitches (no loop left this time) but leaving a few centimetres of thread B sticking out from the end of the stitches.

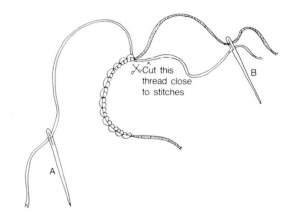

Fig. 63. When joining, the ball thread is pulled through the picot of the ring to be joined (this is where you would use the hook on your needle if you had one) and looped over the needle next to the previous stitch. Then continue with the rest of the stitches as required.

Fig. 65. Now cut the loose end of thread A which you have just taken through the stitches in needle B. Cut it close to the stitches.

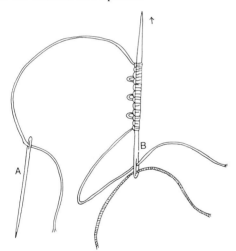

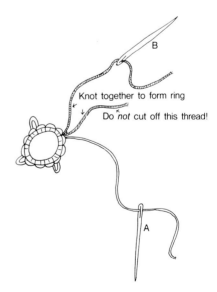

Fig. 64. It is quite simple to work with two colours in your needle tatting. You will need two needles. Thread needle A with one colour and needle B with another colour. They will have to be cut from the balls of thread so make them about thirty centimetres long for practice. Holding needle B, thread the loose end of needle A through the eye and pull a few centimetres through. You now have needle B threaded with two colours and needle A with only one.

Fig. 66. Tie the ends of thread B into a knot, thus forming a ring. Do not cut the loose end of thread B.

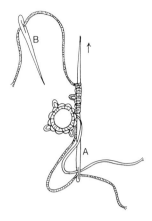

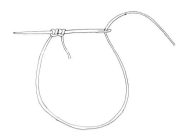

Fig. 67. To make the chain, hold needle A close to the just-made ring and twist thread B around needle A for the required number of stitches. When these have been made, thread the loose end of thread B into needle A and pass needle A through the finished stitches.

Fig. 68. To make a pattern using rings only, a length of thread must be cut from the ball before starting. The needle is threaded and the stitches are formed over the needle using the end of the thread instead of the middle of the thread (see diagram) and then when enough stitches have been made, by sliding them off the needle onto the thread and pulling it up tight a ring is formed just as in normal tatting. (There is no need to tie a knot after making it this time.)

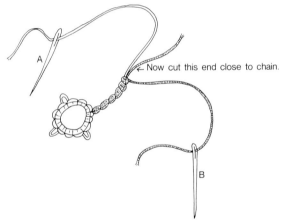

Now cut this end close to chain.

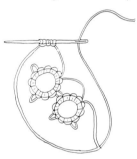

Fig. 67a. The loose end of thread B may now be cut close to the stitches. Push the stitches of the chain up close to the previous ring and you are now ready to continue alternating your colours as you please for rings and chains.

Fig. 68a. Leave a short space and make another ring, making joins in the usual way. The only drawback with making rings-only patterns with a needle is that you must estimate the length of thread required before you start.

Most ordinary patterns may be worked using needle tatting instead of shuttles. Try it, and you'll be surprised how fast you become—especially if you are using a thick needle and wool!

To Make a Chain

Fig. 69. To make a chain instead of a ring, the thread around the hand is taken from a ball of thread, or a second shuttle wound with thread and serving as a ball of thread. (This is explained in the section dealing with using two shuttles, but the principle is the same.)

Just hold the thread from the ball between the thumb and forefinger together with the thread

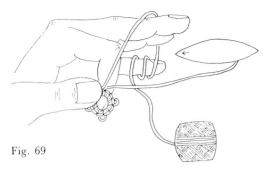

Fig. 69

from the shuttle and then take the ball thread over the back of the hand and wind it around the little finger a couple of times to anchor it. Do not take the shuttle thread round the hand when making a chain.

The stitches are then made in exactly the same way as before, this time with the ball thread forming the stitches over the shuttle thread.

When starting a new piece of tatting with a freshly wound shuttle, don't cut it from the ball of thread after winding it as this will save a join later.

Chains are not usually used to start patterns, therefore you will generally have made a ring before you make a chain. After making the ring the work is reversed (turned upside down) before making the chain and the first stitch of the chain is taken right up close to the base of the ring. The stitches in a chain must still be able to slide on the shuttle thread, although they are not gathered up into a ring—just pushed firmly together before making the next ring.

When the required number of stitches have been made for the chain, the work is reversed again before making the next ring, unless the pattern states otherwise.

Picots

Picots are the decorative little loops which give tatting that extra lacy, delicate look. In reality, they are nothing more than spaces between the stitches.

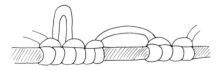

Fig. 70. A picot made and one about to be pushed up.

Fig. 70. To make a picot all you do is leave a short space between the stitch you have just made—a fully completed stitch, not just the first half—and the next stitch you are making. Then

when the ring or chain is finished and the stitches are pulled closed the space slides up to become a loop. The stitches before and after a picot are not counted as a separate item when you are making a pattern. Thus if your pattern reads 'three double stitches, picot, three double stitches' what you actually make is three double stitches, leave a space, three double stitches. If you count the stitch either side of a picot as part of the picot what you would end up with would be *four* double stitches, space, *four* double stitches.

If you wish to make your tatting look even more lacy, make your picots quite long. Alternatively, if you wish it to look plain, leave out all the picots except those needed for joining.

Joining Threads and Getting Rid of Ends

Ideally, on a finished piece of tatting there should be no threads, ends or unwanted knots in sight. However, it is quite surprising the number of people who spend hours making their delicate lace only to tie a knot when they've finished and then cut off the ends and leave little tufts of cotton sticking out of it!

If you have any old pieces of tatting you will know what I mean, as unfortunately tatters used not to be very careful about their finishing-off as a rule.

Nowadays, the majority of tatters tie their final ends in a reef knot, thread the ends into a needle and weave them back into the tatting between the stitches (in opposite directions if there are two threads) (fig. 71).

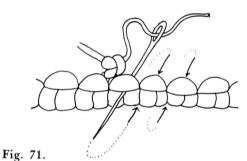

Fig. 71.

While this is a neat way to get rid of ends, it makes a lot of extra sewing when you have to get rid of the ends each time you run out of thread, or if you are making something such as a doily made up of lots of individual motifs.

If you are making something using a ball and shuttle, after filling the shuttle, don't cut the thread. Then, after making your first ring to start your work, you simply reverse your work and there's the ball thread coming out of the ring ready to make the chain.

If your shuttle is not attached to the ball, or if you are using two colours, the best way is to weave in the threads right at the start of your work.

Fig. 72. Wind the shuttle thread around the left hand as normal and make the first half of the

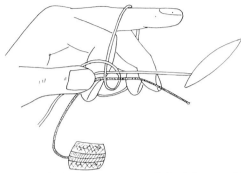

double stitch, but do not pull it tight yet. Now pass the loose end of the ball thread through the loop of the half stitch so that it lies parallel with the shuttle thread.

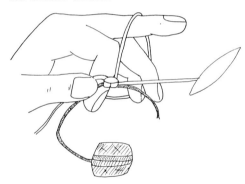

Fig. 73. Make the second half of the stitch, and again pass the loose end through the loop of the stitch with the shuttle thread so that the stitch is actually formed over the two threads.

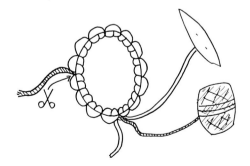

Fig. 74. Repeat this for at least four or five stitches—to make it really neat do so for the entire ring—and then pull the ring tightly closed. Cut the loose end close to the ring.

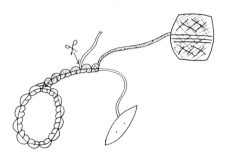

Fig. 75. Now reverse the work to make the chain and this time weave the loose end of the shuttle thread into the chain in the same manner, taking it through at least four or five double stitches—preferably through the whole chain. This may now be cut.

This method may also be used when joining in threads in the middle of your work. It might seem to be fiddly the first time you try it, but it is well worth a little bit of effort to get it right.

If you are making something with only a shuttle, a similar method may be used.

Wind the shuttle thread around the hand to make the first ring and make the first double knot of the ring as normal. Now bring the loose end of the shuttle thread forward and as you are making the first half of the second stitch, pass the loose end through the stitch with the shuttle thread, just as was explained previously. (You must make the first stitch of the ring as usual when using shuttle only to anchor the thread.) Continue weaving the thread through the stitches while making the rest of the ring and then when the ring is tightly closed the loose end may be cut off close to the base of the ring.

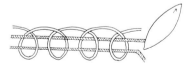

Fig. 76. shows the way the stitches hide the woven-in thread.

To get rid of the final ends when the work is completely finished, a similar method is used which again hides the unwanted ends under the stitches. This may be done in either the final ring, or if a chain is the last to be made, the final chain.

You will need an extra length of thread, preferably slightly finer than the one you are working with. Cut this length into two pieces about fifteen centimetres long. (If you have been using shuttle only you will only need one length of extra thread.)

On your final ring or chain, work it as normal until there are about six or eight stitches still to be made. Now take one of the lengths of cotton and fold it in half to form a loop.

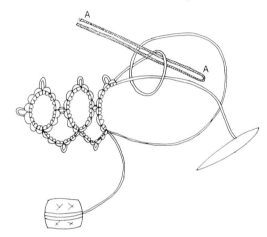

Fig. 77. Weave this loop into the next two stitches in the same manner explained previously for getting rid of ends—that is, through the stitch parallel with the shuttle thread.

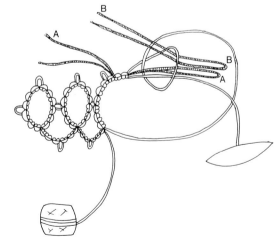

Fig. 78. Now take the other piece of extra thread, fold it into a loop also, and continue weaving *both* loops through the rest of the stitches of the ring or chain. One important thing to

mention here: don't pull the stitches too tight as you are making them over the extra threads.

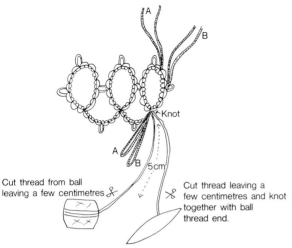

Fig. 79. When the ring or chain has been completely finished, close the ring tightly, or in the case of the chain, tie it to the base of the first ring or chain of the round and then cut both the ball and shuttle threads about five to eight centimetres from the work, and knot them together.

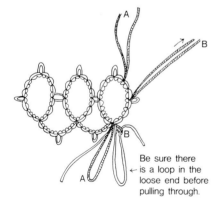

Fig. 80. Now take one of the loose ends (doesn't matter which) and thread just the end of it into the second of the loops you have just woven in (marked B in the diagram). While holding the work steady, gently pull the other end of the loop back through the ring or chain, making sure that there is a loop in the loose end before you try to pull it back through the ring, otherwise it will not pull through.

Fig. 81. This will cause the loose end to be pulled back through the stitches and come out at

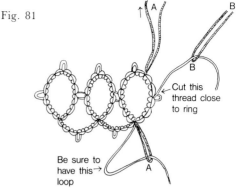

the point where you started weaving the extra loop in.

Do the same with the other loose end, putting it into the first loop (marked A) and again, pulling it gently back through the ring or chain. Now just cut the ends off close to the finished work and you will have a neat, end-less piece of tatting!

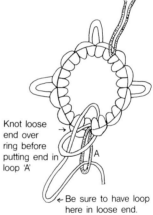

Fig. 82. If you have been using a shuttle only, you will need to weave in one extra thread, as you have only one thread to get rid of.

However, before putting the loose end of the shuttle thread into the extra loop, it *must* be knotted over the space between the first and the last stitch of the ring, otherwise the ring will come undone as you pull the loose end back into it. Try it without knotting first and you will see what I mean.

Like everything else, the more you practice the better you will get at it, so do stick with it, even though at first it might seem like an awful bother. In the long run it will save you hours of extra work!

Joining Rings and Chains Together

Picots, as well as being decorative, are used to join rings and chains together.

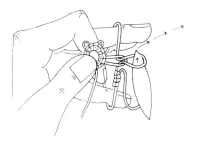

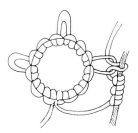

Fig. 84. Hold the stitches and the join and just check that the shuttle thread has not knotted and the stitches still slide as they should. Picots in chains are joined in the same way.

Fig. 83. If your shuttle has a built-in hook on the end or a moulded sharp point this is where it becomes very useful. If your shuttle does not have either of these extras, you will need a small crochet hook to join the picots.

Insert the pointed end of your shuttle (or your crochet hook) through the picot of the ring which is to be joined and pull the ring thread (or ball thread) which passes over the back of your hand, *not* the shuttle thread, through the picot, making a loop large enough to pass the shuttle through. Draw the shuttle through and take the shuttle towards the right as if making an ordinary stitch, at the same time raising the middle finger of the left hand to pull the loop you made back into place. Do not pull this loop too tightly or it could pull the shuttle thread back through the picot which will cause an unwanted knot.

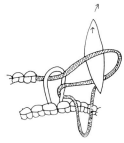

Fig. 85. Sometimes a pattern will call for joins in a chain to be made with the shuttle thread and when this is to be done you must take care that all the stitches prior to the join are pushed up tight, as once the shuttle thread has joined into a picot it will have been knotted and so any stitches before it that are too loose will have to stay that way.

Simple Starter Patterns

Now that the basic technique of tatting has been mastered, obviously the next step is to actually make something.

These next few patterns are all quite easy for beginners and are made with shuttle only—that is to say there are no chains in them. Therefore, after winding the shuttle, the thread may be cut from the ball as the ball thread is not required.

It is better to practise with a fairly thick thread whilst learning as this way you will be able to see what you are doing and how the stitches are formed. If you use a fine crochet cotton you will find it more difficult to do this.

A knitting cotton, especially a variegated colour, is very good for those first tatting efforts.

It's a good idea to make a sample before you start your main work. This will enable you to get used to the pattern and decide what thread is best for your purpose. Keep all these samples in a sample book for future reference. One of the little photo albums with the clear plastic pages would be perfect for this. They are not expensive and can be bought at most department stores.

Remember that you don't have to use an edging or motif only for the purpose given in your pattern. If you see a nice edging and the pattern says it's for a towel—make it in a finer thread and put it round a hankie!

Shuttle Only Patterns

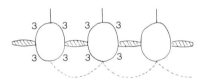

Fig. 86. This is just about the easiest pattern ever. All you do is to make a row of rings joined to each other by side picots. Even though it is so simple, it looks very effective around a hankie.

When you have to leave a short space between rings such as in this pattern and the next one, it is often annoying to get to the end of the piece and find that all the spaces are of different sizes, even when you thought you were being so careful to get them the same!

One way around this problem is to mark your left forefinger with a felt pen or a ball-pen (make sure you remove excess ink from your finger or it will get on your tatting). Make two lines the distance required for your spaces and then as you are working, put the finished ring by one line

and measure the length of thread to the next and start your next ring there. The only problem with this method is that you must renew the lines every time you wash your hands.

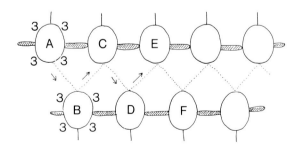

Fig. 87. This pattern is similar to the last except

that the third ring joins to the first and the fourth to the second and so on in a zig-zag fashion. Add extra picots to the rings if you like.

If you make one row of rings slightly larger than the other you will get a curved border.

The patterns in figs 88 to 93 are all done with just the shuttle. If you look at the construction of a pattern it often makes it easier to understand and thus becomes simpler to work. By following the letters A, B, C etc., you will notice that most of the patterns here are worked in a zig-zag.

When going from a ring at the top to a ring at the bottom you will find it easier if you reverse your work. This way, when you come to join to a previous ring you will find that everything is in the right place and no juggling is necessary. After a while you will find that you are automatically reversing without thinking about it.

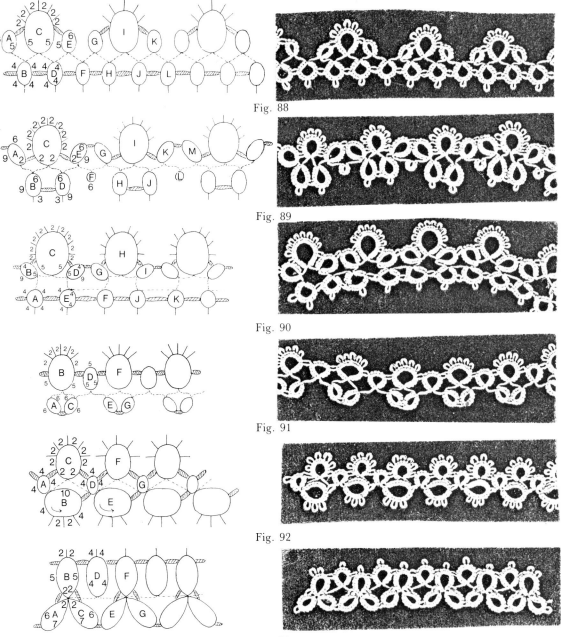

Fig. 88

Fig. 89

Fig. 90

Fig. 91

Fig. 92

Fig. 93

Working with Two Threads

When working a pattern using chains as well as rings a second thread is required and this means having a ball of thread or a second shuttle as well as the usual shuttle.

We will deal with the ball of thread first, as this is the most common way of making a chain.

When filling your shuttle, don't cut it from the ball of thread this time. Start your pattern with a ring, then, having made the ring, reverse the work—turn it upside down—so that the ring now has the top towards the palm of your hand and the closing point of the ring is between your thumb and forefinger. The thread to the ball is coming from the same place.

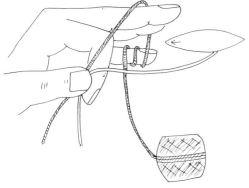

Fig. 94. The thread from the shuttle does not go around the hand while making chains—the thread from the ball forms the stitches. Therefore, take the ball thread (from where it joins the base of the ring just made) over the back of the left hand and wind it around the little finger a couple of times to anchor it.

You will find that after making a ring and before making a chain that you will need to wind some of the slack thread back onto the shuttle. This is because the shuttle thread does not go around the hand. Consequently, when it is time to make the next ring after finishing the chain, you will have to unwind the shuttle thread, and so on.

Now just make your double stitches as before, this time with the thread from the ball making the knots over the shuttle thread. Be sure to make the first knot of the chain right up close to the base of the previous ring (and then, make the following ring right up close to the previous chain).

When you have finished making the chain, it is not pulled up like a ring—just slide the stitches along close to each other so that there are no gaps between them, but not too tightly or the chain will curve too much.

The patterns (figs 95–102) are straightforward and easy to follow as long as you take the time to look at the construction of each pattern before you start.

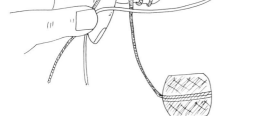

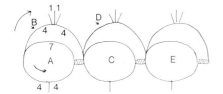

Fig. 95

Fig. 96

41

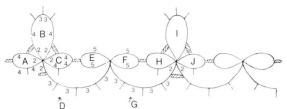

Fig. 97

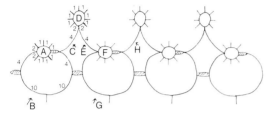

Fig. 98

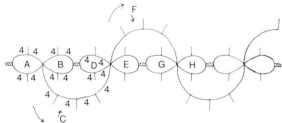

Fig. 99

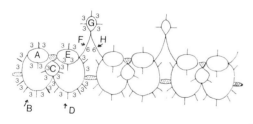

Fig. 100

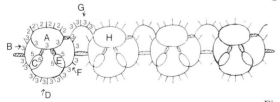

Fig. 101

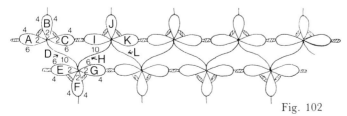

Fig. 102

Tatting with Two Shuttles

Some patterns call for the use of two shuttles, but there is no need to panic if you come across this as the method is exactly the same as using one shuttle and a ball of thread. (When using two shuttles you don't use the ball of thread.)

By having shuttles of different colours it is much easier to see what you are doing, particularly if you have the same colour thread on both shuttles. If you don't have different-coloured shuttles you could mark them in some way—say with a bit of sticky paper—so that you can tell which is which.

In a written pattern the first shuttle is used as the shuttle and the second shuttle is used as the ball of thread, so it is the one used for making the chains, and the thread from it is wound over the back of the left hand to the little finger in the same way that the ball of thread was when you were using it for chains (fig. 103).

One of the most common uses for two shuttles is to make Josephine knots as a decoration on

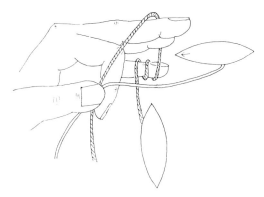

Fig. 103

chains (see next section) but they can also be used if you want to make rings of two colours in the same pattern, such as in the flower pattern which follows (fig. 111). Rings are always the colour of the thread on the shuttle and chains are the colour of the thread on the ball, in case you want to work in two colours. Thus if you want rings of two colours, you will need two shuttles.

Josephine Knots

A Josephine knot is a small ring made up of *either* the first half of the double stitch *or* the second half of the double stitch only (fig. 104).

Fig. 104

Its main function is as decoration on a chain and because of this two shuttles are required if your pattern calls for Josephine knots.

To make one, simply work your chain for the required number of stitches using the two shuttles, then drop the shuttle you have been using as the working shuttle and pick up the shuttle which you have been using as the ball thread. Wind the thread from this second shuttle around your hand as if to make an ordinary ring and make the first half (or the second half, whichever you prefer) of the double stitch and make sure you slide it right up to the chain you have been making. You do *not* reverse your work when making Josephine knots (or when using two shuttles to make rings in the middle of chains) as the Josephine knot has to sit out from the chain along the curve. If you reverse the work it will turn into the inside of the chain and you will lose the effect.

After making the first half-stitch, continue the rest of the ring making the same half of the stitch for as many stitches as required—usually between six and twelve half stitches. Finish it in the normal way by holding the stitches and gently

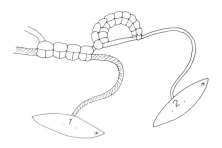

Fig. 105. Josephine ring being made

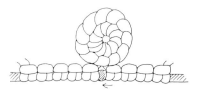

Fig. 106. A finished Josephine ring

pulling the ring closed. You will notice that the Josephine ring (or knot) is a rather flat little ring which looks quite different to an ordinary ring (figs 105, 106).

Therese de Dillmont is credited with inventing the Josephine ring but they were in use long before she wrote her *Encyclopedia of Needlework* in 1886—indeed Riego gives instructions for rings using single knots in the 1850s. Perhaps Mlle de Dillmont gave it the name, but she definitely did not invent it!

Josephine knots (rings or picots—they all mean the same things) are not used very often these days but they can add a slightly different look to a chain without too much extra effort.

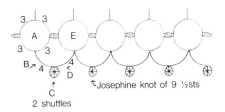

Fig. 107.

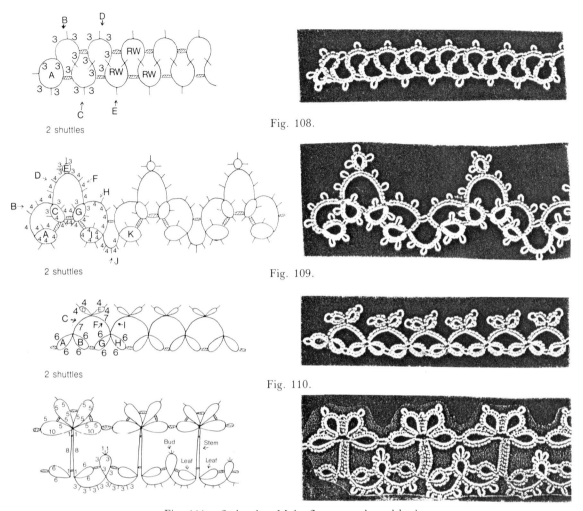

2 shuttles

Fig. 108.

2 shuttles

Fig. 109.

2 shuttles

Fig. 110.

Fig. 111.   2 shuttles. Make flower petals and bud
with one colour and stems and leaves with green.

Motifs

Motifs are simply collections of rings or rings and chains arranged into groups. By joining a number of motifs together you can form doilies, tablemats, tablecloths or even (if you had the patience) bedspreads.

By joining motifs in a straight line you could form a belt. By joining them in a certain order you could make a waistcoat, or a hat, or even a skirt. In fact, you could make anything you want to make. Please don't stop at doilies—go on and make something exciting.

As mentioned in the chapter on the history of tatting, one of the earliest motifs used was the wheel, consisting of a central ring with others around it. There are several different types of wheel and we show some here. (The wheel motif can also be stiffened and used as a Christmas decoration—see the chapter on Christmas tatting.)

Naturally, one of the most popular motifs anyone can make is a flower. The styles are limitless and once you start tatting you will soon be making up your own designs. You can make them with just a shuttle or a shuttle and ball of thread, or even two shuttles.

Some people experience difficulty when joining the last ring of a motif to the first ring, as the picot often becomes twisted in the wrong direction. The solution is really quite simple, especially when you have practised it a few times.

Fig. 112 shows the last ring ready to join to the first. Fold the first ring (A) over to the left so that the back of the ring is facing towards you and the

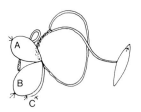

Fig. 113.   First ring (A) folded over to the left so that the back of it is facing towards you and the picot to be joined is sticking out.

picot to be joined is sticking out at the top (fig. 113).

Put the tip of the shuttle (or a fine crochet hook) into the picot *from the back*—that is, the tip comes towards you (fig. 114). Now just catch the

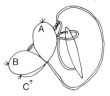

Fig. 114.   Shuttle point (or crochet hook) goes into picot from the *back* towards the front.

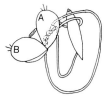

Fig. 115.   The ring thread is caught by the tip of the shuttle and this causes the picot to twist as shown.

ring thread with the tip of the shuttle (fig. 115) and this will cause the picot to twist as shown in the diagram. Pull the ring thread through the picot to form a loop and pass the shuttle through it just as you do when making a normal join (fig. 116).

The loop is then pulled back into place as when making a normal join and the rest of the double stitches are made to complete the ring, which is then closed. Now the motif is pulled into

Fig. 112.   Ready to join last ring of motif to first ring (A).

shape and the ends are finished off neatly as usual.

You will see that the picot is now the right way round and the last ring has fitted in tidily.

Figs 117–123 show motifs made with a shuttle only. Figs 124–128 show motifs made with shuttle and the ball of thread. After making the whole motif of rings and chains, it is finished off by tying the last chain to the base of the first ring.

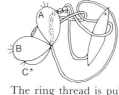

Fig. 116. The ring thread is pulled through the twisted picot to form a loop and the shuttle passes through this loop as in a normal join. The ring thread loop is pulled back into place and the ring is completed as normal.

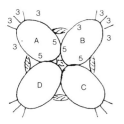

Fig. 117. Shuttle only

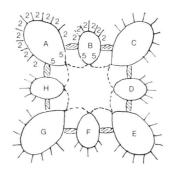

Fig. 120. Shuttle only

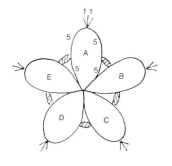

Fig. 118. Shuttle only

Fig. 121. Shuttle only

Fig. 119. Shuttle only

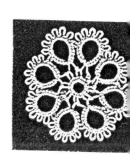

Fig. 122. Shuttle only

47

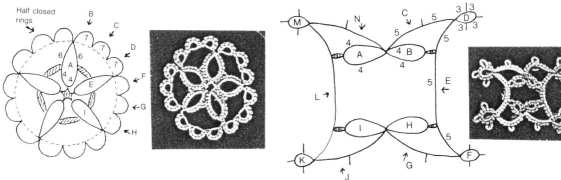

Fig. 123. Shuttle only

Fig. 126

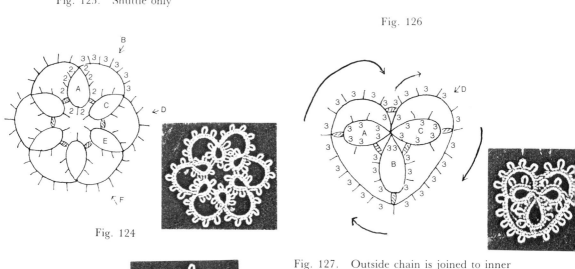

Fig. 124

Fig. 127. Outside chain is joined to inner cloverleaf by the shuttle thread.

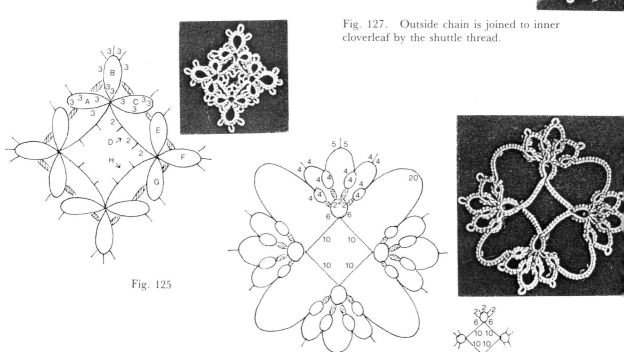

Fig. 125

Fig. 128. Make inner motif first

Ric-rac Tatting

Ric-rac tatting is also known as zig-zag tatting or sets of stitches and those who have read Elgiva Nicholls' books will know it as node stitch.

It is very easy to work, being simply the first half of the double stitch worked a certain number of times—say four times—and then the second half of the double stitch worked the same number of times. The stitches are then pulled along the shuttle thread fairly firmly which gives you the zig-zag effect (fig. 129).

Fig. 129

It was very popular in America at the beginning of this century, but didn't catch on much anywhere else. In some books published recently which reprint old American patterns, the method is called sets of stitches and in the pattern is written as follows:

Sets of sts 4–4 (or 3–3, or any other numbers may be used). This means that the first half of the stitch is worked four times and then the second half is worked four times. This is one set. The pattern may say, for example, 3 sets 4–4. This means that the complete set is worked three times.

Ric-rac tatting may be worked in rings or chains and picots may be added either at the end of each set (which will make all the picots on one side of the work) or in the middle of a set and at the end which will give you picots on both sides of the work.

In most patterns using ric-rac tatting either only the rings or only the chains are worked in this manner, as by reversing the work the zig-zag changes sides and this gives a rather untidy look to the work.

You can convert some regular tatting patterns to use the zig-zag and it looks particularly effective in a pattern which has a row of individually made flower motifs.

Elgiva Nicholls, while basically using sets of stitches, calls her method node stitch and has the zig-zags at the back of the work instead of the front so that the finished article looks smooth with little bumps or 'nodes' poking out from under the work (fig. 130), whereas ordinary ric-rac tatting has a rippled look to it caused by the stitches changing direction.

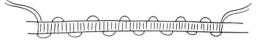

Fig. 130

Another slightly different effect can be made with chains made by working only one half of the double stitch throughout—as with the Josephine knot, *either* the first half of the stitch *or* the second half. This will give a twisted spiral look to the chain which, while not being very useful, is something further to experiment with (fig. 131).

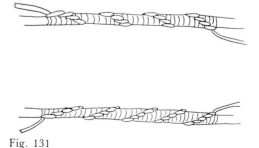

Fig. 131

Lock Stitch

The vast majority of tatting patterns start with a ring, thus giving you something firm to hold on to before making a chain, but occasionally you may come across a pattern which requires you to start with a chain (such as some of the bookmarks shown elsewhere in this book) and this can be very awkward unless you know the easy way to do it.

If the pattern starts with just a chain (no tassels as in a bookmark) and the shuttle is joined to the ball thread already, start to make the normal first half of the double stitch. *However*, now we go against everything you have struggled to learn about getting the stitch to click onto the right thread, because instead of keeping the shuttle thread nice and straight this time the first half of the stitch must be formed with the ball thread being straight and the shuttle thread making the loop. After finally learning the correct way to form the stitch, you may even find it a bit difficult to make it go the other way, but it is necessary.

As you slide this wrong-way half stitch along to the end loop of the thread, slip a pin into the loop as shown in fig. 132 as this will give you something to hold on to while commencing your chain.

Now make the second half of the stitch as normal and proceed with the rest of your pattern. By making the knot with the shuttle thread you have prevented the chain from pulling up too tight into a curve.

If making a tassel at the start of a chain such as in the bookmarks, leave long threads (for the tassel) before making the lock stitch and make it in exactly the same way. However, you won't need the pin as you have the long ends to hold on to.

Another use for the lock stitch is to make a false picot. This can be used as a method of getting from the first ring of your pattern to the next row, if the next row starts with a chain joined into a picot of the first row. By making a false picot you avoid the need to make a join. (The shuttle should still be joined to the ball.)

Make the ring as usual but do not make the last picot in the pattern. Instead, leave a space the length of the other picots on the shuttle thread and the ball thread and make a lock stitch as shown in fig. 133.

Make the space between the ring and the lock stitch the same size as picots

Fig. 133

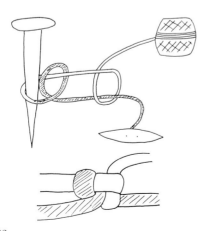

Fig. 132

Fig. 134

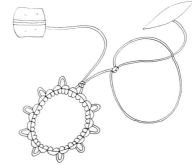

Fig. 135

Now make the chain as required, counting the lock stitch as the first stitch of the sequence (fig. 134).

If the second row of the pattern has a ring joined to the first ring, make the lock stitch as explained above, but then leave another short space on the shuttle thread, equivalent to the diameter of the ring to be made, and then make the first stitch of the ring (fig. 135).

Make the ring as normal until you come to the picot where it must join into the first ring, then make that join over the lock stitch, finish off the second ring and close it (fig. 136). There will be the short space of thread across the back of the ring but this will not show much on the finished work.

To make the first chain of the second row, just carry the ball thread across the ring (on the same side as the other thread) and without pulling it too tightly, make your chain (fig. 137).

This is called slip-stitching and with a little practice, you can soon estimate more or less the right length of thread to leave before starting the next ring or chain.

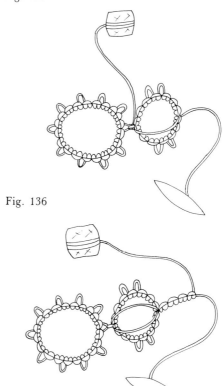

Fig. 136

Fig. 137

Re-opening a Closed Ring

One of the drawbacks to tatting is that if you make a mistake, unlike knitting or crochet, you cannot just pull a thread and it comes undone. Unfortunately, it has to be unpicked, very carefully, half stitch by half stitch.

A chain is unpicked fairly easily by using one of those little hem-unpickers or even a pin, but you must be careful not to fray the thread while doing it.

A ring, however, is quite a different matter.

Most people say you can't open a ring once it has been closed on a mistake, but with a bit of care and practice, it can be done.

If the offending ring has picots, carefully catch up the shuttle thread by inserting the point of your shuttle or a very fine crochet hook into the loop of the last picot of the ring (fig. 138). Once you have eased a short length of the shuttle thread out, move on to the next picot. Pull the shuttle thread out of this picot and slide the stitches between it and the last picot in a clockwise direction (fig 139) until you get around to the first picot of the ring. You should now, by holding the last part of the ring firmly but gently, be able to slide the first few stitches along the pulled-out shuttle thread. Gently pull the shuttle thread back through the stitches in an anti-clockwise direction, thus opening up the ring fully to correct any mistakes (fig. 140).

It is not advisable to try to undo a ring by unpicking it stitch by stitch without first re-opening it, as nine times out of ten you only cause a worse mess than you had to start with.

As a last resort, it is better to cut the mistake right out leaving ends, which can then be woven in when the new thread is joined in.

By the way, if the ring you wish to unpick does not have any picots, just ease your unpicker carefully between two stitches until you can catch the shuttle thread and then proceed as explained previously.

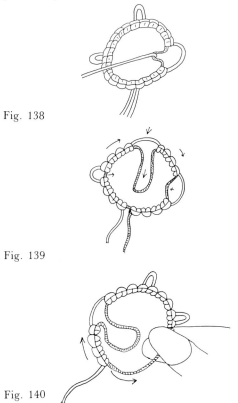

Fig. 138

Fig. 139

Fig. 140

Pearl Tatting and Tatting with Three Threads

In Victorian times picots were called 'pearls' or 'purls' and pearl tatting is a method of tatting which, although not making true picots, forms little loops which look like picots.

This is achieved by using two ball threads and making the double stitches in them alternately. To practice, have threads of different colours— say red and blue. The colour of the shuttle thread doesn't matter as it won't show.

Tie the two ball threads and the shuttle thread together. Wind both the red and the blue threads around the little finger and over the back of the hand in the usual way to make chains, but just keep the threads a bit apart as they have to be worked separately (fig. 141).

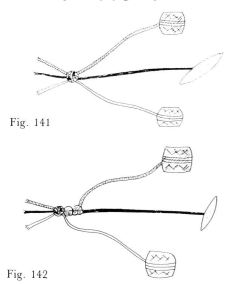

Fig. 141

Fig. 142

Make two double stitches with the red thread (fig. 142). Now reverse the work and make two double stitches with the blue thread. Again reverse the work (making sure that the shuttle thread does not get tangled with the ball threads) and make two more stitches with the red thread. The little loop formed between each group of

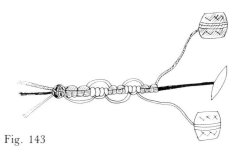

Fig. 143

stitches of the same colour will make the so-called pearls (fig. 143). If you have a minimum amount of thread between each group you will have very small pearls, but if you leave a long loop between, naturally you will have quite long picots.

By varying the number of stitches and adding true picots to the groups of each colour, some quite interesting patterns may be made.

For example, make two double stitches, three picots, and two more double stitches in red. Reverse the work and make three double stitches, one picot and three double stitches with the blue thread (fig. 144). Continue in this way for the length required.

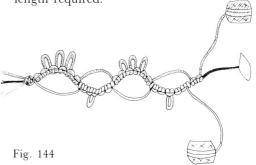

Fig. 144

This method of using two ball threads and a shuttle was often used by early tatters to made a padded cord either for trimming or decoration instead of buying a commercially made one.

Wind the shuttle with three or four strands of cotton instead of the usual one strand. Now make the pearl tatting as explained above. You will see that now the little pearls sit either side of a thick cord. Other tatting may be attached to the pearls, or this could be used as an insertion between two pieces of material, etc (fig. 145).

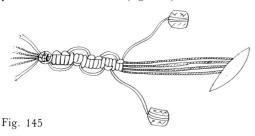

Fig. 145

Of course, you could use more than just the two extra ball threads—try using four or even six, picking up each in turn, three to a side. It wouldn't really be practical to use too many, but at least you could say you had tried!

Going back to our three threads (two ball threads and a shuttle thread), another variation is to wind the two ball threads on to extra shuttles. This gives you the opportunity to make

rings or Josephine rings on either side of the original pearl chain (fig. 146).

Fig. 146

Cluny Tatting

Although this is a rather time-consuming and not really practical method of tatting, it is worth mentioning because you can achieve some quite nice effects with it.

It is actually a form of weaving, using the tatting shuttle to make little tallies similar to those seen in bobbin lace. There are very few patterns available; in fact, I have only ever seen one in print, many years ago in an American magazine.

However, I have designed a small motif which could be made into a place-mat or some such thing by joining several together.

Before attempting the motif, make a few practice tallies just to get the hang of it. Once you get used to the way the threads are pulled to form the tally after weaving with your shuttle, it is not really very hard, only a bit fiddly.

Both the ball of thread and the shuttle are required and it's a good idea to tie them together if they are not already joined and work a small ring to give you something to hold on while you are working the tally.

Motif made in Cluny tatting (see fig. 158)

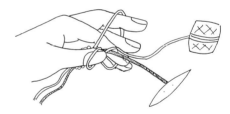

Fig. 148. Carry the ball thread around the thumb (this is just to anchor the thread) and under the shuttle thread. Take the thread over the forefinger and between the middle finger and the ring finger.

Fig. 147. Hold the ring between the thumb and forefinger of the left hand and take the ball thread over the middle and ring finger and then between the ring finger and the little finger and back between the thumb and forefinger, letting it fall towards you over the thumb.

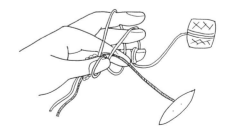

Fig. 149. Pass the thread over the ring finger and wind it around the little finger several times to secure it.

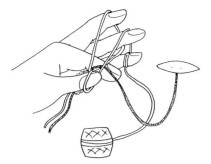

Fig. 150. You are now ready to start the tally.

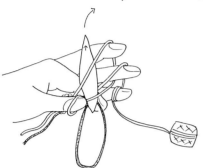

Fig. 151. Make one double stitch on the first thread—the one going over the middle finger—and then weave the shuttle under the right hand thread, over the middle thread and under the left hand (first) thread.

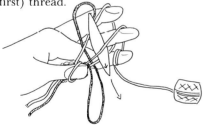

Fig. 152. Now bring the shuttle back again, this time doing the opposite—going over the first and third threads and under the middle one.

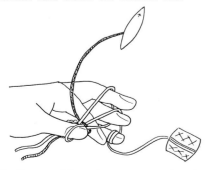

Fig. 153. Repeat this action ten or twelve times,

making sure the first stitches are well down close to the thumb and forefinger at the beginning of the tally.

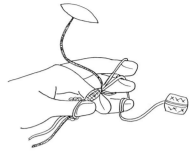

Fig. 154. Make the first couple of stitches quite narrow and gradually increase the width by about the fourth stitch. Decrease the size at about the ninth stitch so that an oval shape is obtained. If ten stitches are used the tally is rather stubby, but twelve stitches make rather a nice oval shape.

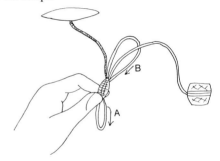

Fig. 155. Unwind the ball thread from the little finger and remove all the other loops from the fingers, holding the tally between the thumb and forefinger. Gently pull the right hand side of the bottom loop (the one which was around the thumb) downwards (marked A in fig. 155).

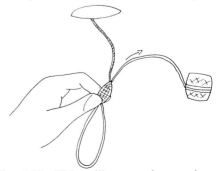

Fig. 156. This will cause the top loop (B) to disappear and loop A will get bigger.

56

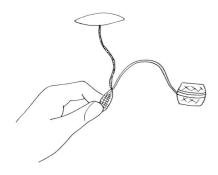

Fig. 157. Now gently pull the ball thread which is coming from the top of the tally upwards. This will make the bottom loop disappear and give you the completed tally. Make a double stitch as normal close to the end of the tally as this will keep it firm.

So you see, it wasn't really very difficult, was it? But do make a few practice tallies, maybe even using a thick thread just to be sure which threads to pull when finishing it off. The key word here is *gently*. If you pull too hard or jerk the thread you could end up with a knot and have to start all over again.

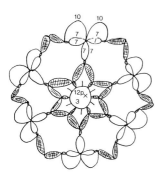

Fig. 158

To make the motif (fig. 158) using tallies, start with a ring of twelve picots separated by three double stitches.

The second row is all tallies and is best made with a freshly wound shuttle still attached to the ball thread, thus avoiding joins. If you have them separated you can sew the ends into the tally when it is completed.

Join the thread to any picot on the first ring and make a double stitch. Now make a tally of twelve stitches and finish with a double stitch. Make a second tally the same, and join into the second picot from the one you started with. Make one double stitch. This will give you two tallies looking like an inverted V joined to two picots of the original ring with an unattached picot between them.

Continue around the first ring in this manner until you have six inverted Vs and join the last tally into the base of the first (fig. 158). Tie the ends and sew them back into a tally.

The outer row has cloverleaves between the tallies so start by making a cloverleaf of three rings each of seven double stitches, one picot, seven double stitches and join the picot of the middle ring to the point of the inverted V between the two tallies.

Make a chain of ten double stitches and join into the picot of the third ring. Make one double stitch followed by a tally. Make the second tally in the same way as you did on the previous row.

Make another chain of ten double stitches and then another cloverleaf, joining into the base of the last tally at the point where the chain starts. Continue as before joining each cloverleaf point into the previous row of tallies. Join the final chain into the middle of the first cloverleaf.

Roll Tatting

Roll Tatting is a novelty which emerged in the 1920s, but did not last very long.

It is just what the name implies—the ring thread is rolled around the shuttle thread several times and this gives a smooth but twisted effect to your work.

Nearly all conventional patterns can be adapted to roll tatting without much effort.

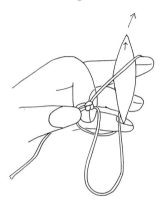

Fig. 159. To start a ring, wind the thread around the hand and make the first double stitch in the usual manner. Now, with a loop from the thread between the shuttle and the first stitch hanging downwards, pass the shuttle *under* the ring thread and away to the right. You do not make a knot of any kind. Keep the shuttle thread taut and straight as you do with normal tatting and this will cause the ring thread to twist around it.

10 times—making sure that the shuttle thread is kept straight at all times. Keep the rolled stitches between the thumb and forefinger to keep them in position.

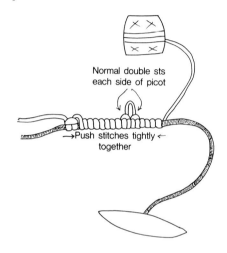

Fig. 161. To make a picot, push the rolled stitches tightly back up to the first double stitch you made and then make an ordinary double stitch. Leave a space for the picot and then make another ordinary double stitch. Now continue with your rolled stitches as before.

That's all there is to it! At the end of every ring or chain you must make an ordinary double stitch to hold the rolled stitches in place. Try it with an easy pattern first to get the hang of it.

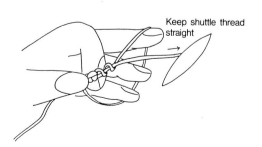

Fig. 160. Repeat this action several times—say

Tatting with Beads

Although beads are not used very often these days in tatting, now and again you may like to use them when making a pair of tatted earrings or perhaps to add a decorative touch to a tatted Christmas bell.

There are a couple of different methods of adding beads to tatting, depending on where you want to place them.

The simplest method of all is to include them in a chain. First count how many beads are required for the piece of work and then thread them onto the ball thread before starting the chain. Then as the pattern calls for a bead to be used, you just slide one up as close as possible to the previous stitch and make the next double stitch right up close to the bead (fig. 162). When beads are used they are usually in place of picots.

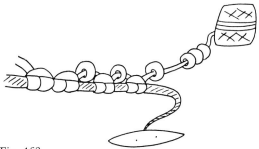

Fig. 162

If you wish to use beads in the ring where that ring is not joined to another, then the beads must be threaded onto the shuttle thread and wound on to the shuttle with the thread. This is rather an awkward operation as the beads never seem to be where you need them when you need them! However, it can be done.

Suppose you wish to make a ring with five beads with three double stitches between them. Wind off the five beads from the shuttle and be sure they are on the length of thread which goes around your hand. Keep the beads away from the working area of the ring—that is to say near your thumb and towards the palm of your hand. Make your first three stitches as normal and then slide

the first bead along to the last stitch. Make the next three stitches being sure to make the first one right up close to the bead.

Continue this until the ring is finished and pull it closed in the usual way (fig. 163). If you have

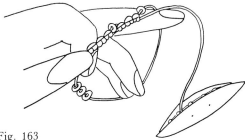

Fig. 163

to make a chain between rings, just make sure that no unwanted beads get unwound from the shuttle while you are doing it. Then when you come to another ring, you proceed as before.

When beads are used between rings or between rings and chains either of the previous methods may be used but there is a better one.

The beads are incorporated into the tatting by threading long picots through them and then joining the picots as normal to the next ring or chain. This avoids having to thread beads onto either shuttle or ball thread and thus makes the work easier.

Make the first ring as usual but make the picot which is to carry the bead as long as the bead plus a little bit extra (fig. 164). You will now have

Fig. 164

a ring, normal-sized picots and one (or more) extra long picots.

Depending on the size of the hole in the bead either put it on the end of a fine crochet hook and put the hook through the picot and slide the bead off the hook and onto the picot (fig. 165). Once

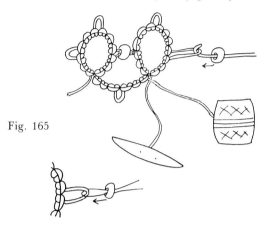

Fig. 165

Fig. 165a

in place, slip a pin through the end of the picot to hold the bead until you are ready to make the join (fig. 166).

If the hole in the bead is too fine to fit on a crochet hook, thread a short length of sewing cotton through the picot and then thread both ends through the bead. The bead will then slide easily on to the picot (fig. 165a) and can be held in place with a pin.

When the next ring is ready to be joined to the first with the bead between them, just remove the pin and make your join in the normal way into the short end of the picot which sticks out from the bead (fig. 167).

Naturally it will take a little practice to master these methods and join the beads in neatly and easily, but like everything, it's worth the little extra effort to do it, even though you may not need it very often.

Fig. 166

Fig. 167

Tatting Round Hankies

One of the questions I get asked most frequently is : 'How do I fix my tatting onto a handkerchief?' and there is no official answer.

Absolute traditionalists say that you must make a length of tatting first, the same size as the hankie it is to fit, and then neatly sew it round by catching each picot with a fine thread running through the hem of the hankie (fig. 168).

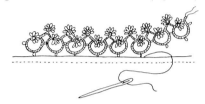

Fig. 168. Tatting is made first, then sewn to hankie

The main problem with this method is that so often the pattern has to be varied at each corner so that the extra fullness needed to get around the corner can be worked in, and unless you measure each side very carefully you could be in trouble when you come to join the tatting on.

The best way to get around this is to work a few centimetres of tatting and then stitch that to the hankie. Now work a few more centimetres more and again stitch it to the hankie. This way you know exactly where the corner will come and can fit it in perfectly.

The next method is to crochet around the hankie (after making either the full length of tatting or just a few centimetres at a time) and catch the picots with a crocheted slip-stitch as you go (Fig. 169).

Fig. 169. Make the tatting first and catch the bottom picot with a slip stitch as you crochet round the hankie

By making the tatting first and then joining it to the hankie by the picots you get a lacy effect

caused by the space between the tatted edging and the hankie.

Another way to edge a hankie is to tat directly on to it. This way you know just when your corner is coming up and can adjust accordingly. The edging will be firmer and less lacy as there will be no space between the tatting and the hankie.

Again, there are several ways to do this.

If you like to crochet, you can crochet all round the hankie first and then tat into the crocheted edge. This will give a very firm edge (fig. 170).

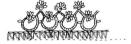

Fig. 170. Crochet round hankie first, then tat into the crochet

The joins into the crochet are made in the same way as the join between two picots in tatting—that is, by pulling the ring thread through the hankie with a fine crochet hook, and then passing your shuttle through the loop which has been formed, and then carry on as usual (fig. 171).

Fig. 171. How to join the tatting into the crochet

If you don't want to crochet round the hankie you can tat straight into the edge of it. The joins are made in the same way as described above.

The easiest way to do this is to make a border of chains (fig. 172). To start this it is best to have

Fig. 172. Tatting a border of chains directly onto hankie

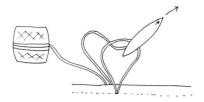

Fig. 173. How to join thread to hankie before starting chain border

the shuttle freshly wound and still attached to the ball of thread. Pull a thread through one of the holes in the hem of the hankie and pass the shuttle through it (fig. 173), and then pull the thread back into place. Continue with your pattern for the required number of stitches until the next join is needed.

With a chain pattern such as this, the joins are made with the *shuttle* thread and not the thread around your hand (fig. 174).

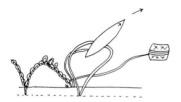

Fig. 174. Joining into hankie whilst working border

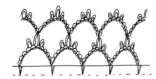

Fig. 175. A second row added to the first row of chains

If desired, a second row of tatting may be added after the first has been completed (fig. 175).

To join an edging consisting of just rings or rings and chains directly to the hankie, the joins are made with the *ring* thread, *not* the shuttle thread (fig. 176).

When joining directly to the hankie, if the thread used is the same colour as the hankie, the threads making the join will not show very much

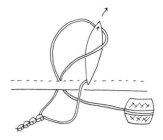

Fig. 176. Joining a border directly to a hankie

Fig. 177. Border joined directly onto hankie

(fig. 177), but if a contrasting colour is used then there will be stitches showing across the hem of the hankie.

One way to get around this problem is to make your edging a two-coloured border and have one colour on your shuttle (for the rings) and the same colour as the hankie on the ball of thread as this will make your joins across the hem of the hankie the same colour and thus less noticeable (fig. 178). Of course, if you are joining to the

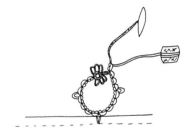

Fig. 178

hankie by the rings and not the chains, put the hankie colour on the shuttle and not the ball.

Always make the joins evenly spaced by counting the number of holes between each join. A good idea is to count along to the end of the side of the hankie you are working on when you are about two thirds of the way along, just in case the holes don't work out evenly. This way you can make allowances by adding or subtracting extra holes between joins.

Moving on

Now that you have mastered the art of tatting (wasn't really that hard, was it?), made a few edgings round hankies, joined a few motifs together and made some doilies—you may even have dusted off grandma's old doily and had a go at copying it—what can you do next?

This might be called the parting of the ways, although I don't think it is. The traditionalists will carry on making doilies and hankies, but if you use your imagination you will realise that a whole new world of tatting awaits you.

The next sections cover the more unusual and even unexpected side of tatting. Don't think that they are projects for advanced tatters only—once you can make that knot correctly and can join without twisting your picots, you can make anything you want to.

There is one point to make about the diagrams. Because some of the items are round or shaped, such as the bell or the basket, and the diagrams are, naturally, flat, some of the picots look very long and out of proportion in some places, but they are all normal-sized picots unless otherwise stated and the pattern continues right round the subject even though only a section has been shown.

With the tatted notepaper, the tatted flowers have been drawn in to give an idea of how to place them, but when you make your own sketches for your notepaper just draw the stems without the flowers and stick on the tatted ones.

The doodles can also be used on notepaper or on place cards for children's parties, or even on the collar of a child's dress or shirt.

To fix tatting (of any kind) directly onto material such as flowers in the corner of hankies or on to blouses, instead of stitching them on (which leaves stitches showing on the other side no matter how neat you are) try using one of the special glues used to put up the hems of skirts and dresses. Just dab it on to the back of the tatting with a toothpick, place it where it has to go, put a piece of cloth over the tatting and iron it firmly. You can also use the fusible webbing for this purpose.

With normal washing it won't come off, and it is much easier than sewing tatting into place.

Remember, tatting is fun and I hope you have fun and enjoyment from making some of these more unusual items.

Tatted Notepaper

A very inexpensive idea for last-minute gifts is to make your own exclusive stationery.

Using a matching pad and envelopes of your choice, all you do is draw a little sketch or a few lines to represent stems in the top left-hand corner of each page and stick on a couple of tatted flowers. Add another on the bottom left-hand corner of the envelope and you're in business!

All you need to make the sketches are a couple of fine-point felt pens—the number depends on how detailed your drawings are to be. If you choose only to draw a few straight lines with leaves on them, then you'll only need a green pen. The background of the sketch may be coloured with coloured pencils as this gives a soft look, but water colour paints are just as good.

In the examples shown the flowers have been drawn in to give an idea of how to place them, but when you do your own, draw your sketch without the flowers and place them where you like.

Use a clear hobby glue to stick the flowers on to the notepaper. I put a dob of glue on to some scrap paper and dab it on to the back of the flower with a toothpick while holding the flower with tweezers, but you'll soon find the method most convenient to you.

The flowers are made in long 'daisy' chains and are nothing more that a ring with five or seven picots separated by one double stitch. If you use fine crochet cotton the flowers are a bit thin looking but a size 10 crochet cotton would be suitable if you have it. Coats or Semco broder cotton (not the stranded embroidery cotton) is ideal as it comes in such a huge range of colours and is relatively cheap, so you can buy as many different colours as you want.

For Christmas cards or gift tags draw holly leaves and use red cotton for the flowers. Add red berries to the leaves with felt pen and stick some glitter dust around the flowers to give the finishing touch.

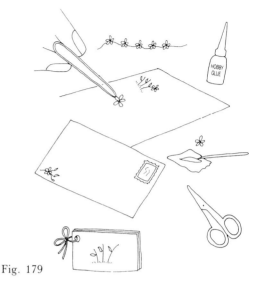

Fig. 179

After making your daisy chain of flowers, cut them off close to the base of the flower for use (fig. 179). Put a dab of hobby glue on the centre back of each flower and also on the tip of each petal and then just press into position.

Designs can be very simple—you don't have to be an artist, or even be able to draw a straight line. Just draw any line—straight or otherwise—and add another wiggle for a leaf and then stick on your flower!

Make a little reference book of your different designs by putting each little sketch on to a separate card, such as those little visiting cards obtainable from newsagents. Punch a hole in the corner and run a thread through and then you'll have them all together and can add to them whenever you get fresh ideas (figs 180–196).

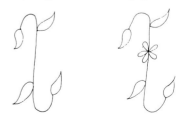

Fig. 180. Sketch before and after the flower is added

Did you know that Vermeer's 'Lacemaker' had a twin sister who liked to tat? Her lace bobbins are gone and she now uses a large silver shuttle to make her lace.

Tatted hankies always make a very acceptable gift. Make them all year round and they will be ready when you need them.

Tatted notepaper is quick and easy to make. Make the flowers in long daisy-chains and cut them off as you need them.

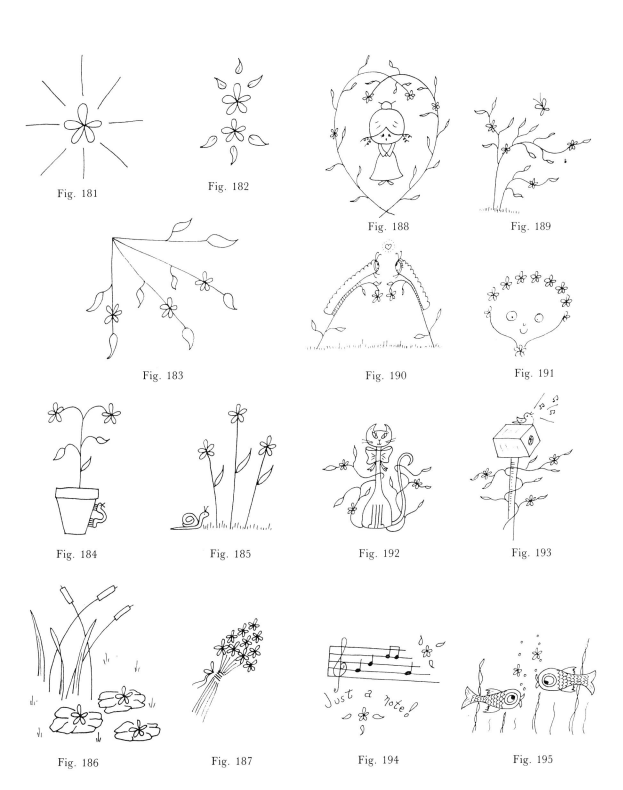

Fig. 181

Fig. 182

Fig. 188

Fig. 189

Fig. 183

Fig. 190

Fig. 191

Fig. 184

Fig. 185

Fig. 192

Fig. 193

Fig. 186

Fig. 187

Fig. 194

Fig. 195

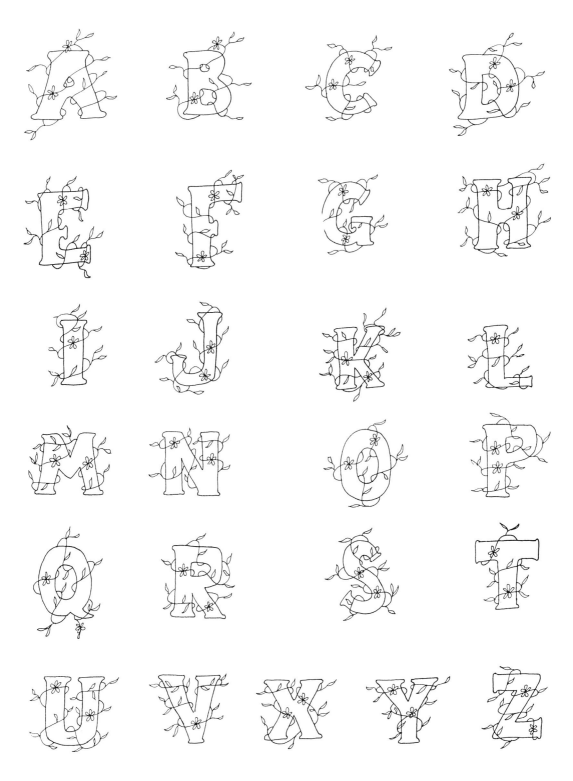

Fig. 196

Tatted Bookmarks

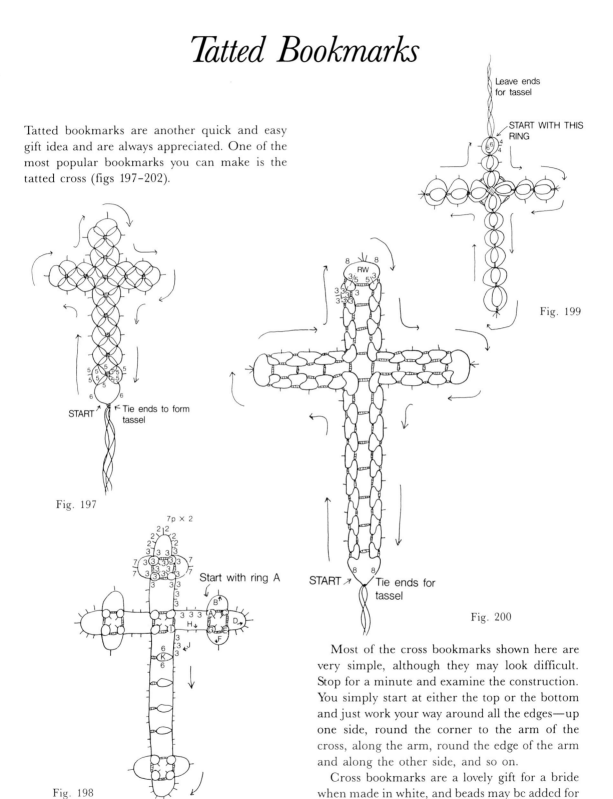

Tatted bookmarks are another quick and easy gift idea and are always appreciated. One of the most popular bookmarks you can make is the tatted cross (figs 197–202).

Leave ends for tassel

START WITH THIS RING

Fig. 199

START Tie ends to form tassel

Fig. 197

7p × 2

Start with ring A

Fig. 198

RW

START Tie ends for tassel

Fig. 200

Most of the cross bookmarks shown here are very simple, although they may look difficult. Stop for a minute and examine the construction. You simply start at either the top or the bottom and just work your way around all the edges—up one side, round the corner to the arm of the cross, along the arm, round the edge of the arm and along the other side, and so on.

Cross bookmarks are a lovely gift for a bride when made in white, and beads may be added for

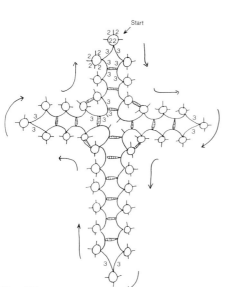

Start

Fig. 201

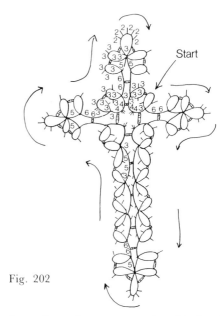

Start

Fig. 202

further attraction. You can easily make a complete rosary.

As well as the crosses, other kinds of bookmarks can also be made. How about an anchor, a flower, or one made from a favourite edging which has been adapted slightly (figs 203–207).

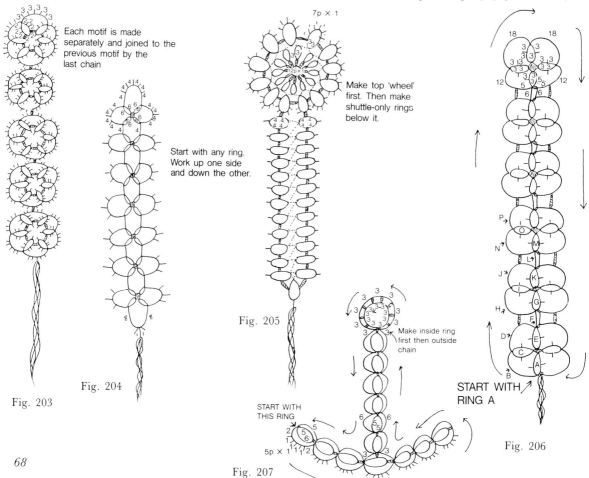

Each motif is made separately and joined to the previous motif by the last chain

Start with any ring. Work up one side and down the other.

Make top 'wheel' first. Then make shuttle-only rings below it.

Fig. 205

Fig. 204

Fig. 203

Make inside ring first then outside chain

START WITH THIS RING

5p × 1

Fig. 207

START WITH RING A

Fig. 206

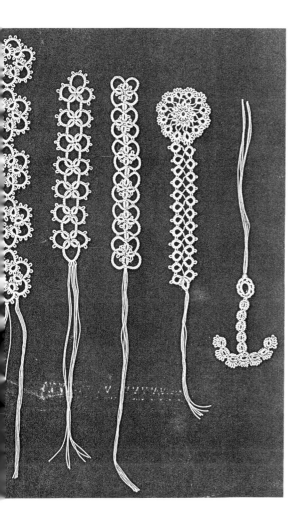

Tatted bookmarks—always an appreciated gift.

Tatted Butterflies

One of the most attractive forms of tatting is tatted butterflies. Not only can they be used to decorate hankies, blouses and other items of clothing, but also to decorate your home. For instance, why not make different-sized and different-coloured butterflies and fix them around a lampshade? Or stiffen them and make a mobile for a child's bedroom? Or stick them to little magnets and make 'fridgies' to stick on your fridge door? The ideas are endless!

The butterfly border (fig. 208) is really simple and quick, as the ends do not have to be sewn or

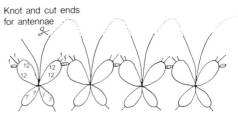

Fig. 208

woven in. Just leave a few centimetres of thread before you start, make your four rings for the wings and then tie the beginning thread and the last thread together in a knot, making sure that

Tatted butterflies. Use them to decorate anything from clothing to stationery. Stiffen them and make mobiles.

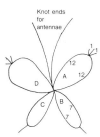

Fig. 209

the two large rings are pulled close together. Then you can either cut the ends to form antennae and leave it at that to form a single butterfly (fig. 209), or leave a few more centimetres of thread and make a second butterfly, joining them together as shown in the diagram. The ends can then be cut when you have finished the required length of your border.

Alternatively, a very pretty effect can be obtained by using several different colours and joining them together as a border.

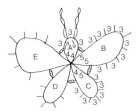

Fig. 210

The next butterfly (fig. 210) is similar to the first but has a head and long picots are twisted to form the antennae. Start with ring A and work all

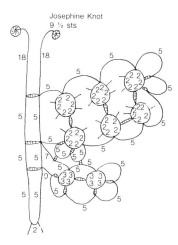

Fig. 211

round finishing with ring E. The ends are then taken behind the work, knotted and sewn in neatly.

The butterfly in fig. 211 has Josephine knots on the antennae, as do most of the others shown here.

Start with the body at the first Josephine knot, and weave in the end of your thread whilst making it. Make the long chain for the rest of the body and join it together as you come up the other side.

Next make the top wing followed by the bottom wing. Cut and tie the threads and repeat the same on the other side. Only one side has been shown in the pattern as they are both the same.

With the next butterfly the method of making is slightly different. Make the top wing (A) first, then the bottom one (B), joining it to A. Cut and tie the threads. The body is made in two pieces, starting with the Josephine knot at the top (weave in ends again) then the wings are joined by the shuttle thread as you go and picots are made on the first side of the body (C) so that the second side may be attached. Leave a few centimetres at the end of the body as the two ends are tied together to form the tail (fig. 212).

The other side of the butterfly is made in the same way—wings first, then the body. This time the body chain is joined into the picots made on the first side of the body.

You will notice that the next butterfly (fig. 213) is based on the little heart-shaped motif shown earlier. Again, it has the Josephine knot antennae. First make the whole body, then the top wing, joining to the body as you go. The bottom wing is actually half the same motif as the top one, and part of the large ring is hidden behind the top wing. Join as shown in the diagram and then cut and tie the ends. Make the other side to correspond with the first.

The last butterfly (fig. 214) has a different body, which is made first. Leave long ends to form the antennae. The rest of the butterfly can be made all in one go by following the direction of the arrows in the diagram.

Start with wing A, joining your thread at the picot between the head and the body, making your chain as shown, joining back into the same place. Next make a short chain down to the first available picot on the body, and then continue as shown by the arrows (B). This chain joins on to the top wing of chain A and then turns on itself and crosses over itself (take on thread either side of chain B) to become chain D and this goes back to the same picot that chain B began from.

The bottom wing, chain E, comes down from this same picot and after making it, it joins into the picot between the second and third rings of the body. After joining into this picot, take one thread either side of the body and make a join into the corresponding picot on the other side of the body. You are now ready to make the second side of the butterfly, only this time in reverse. All

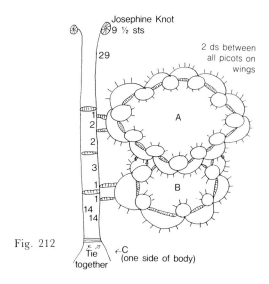

Fig. 212

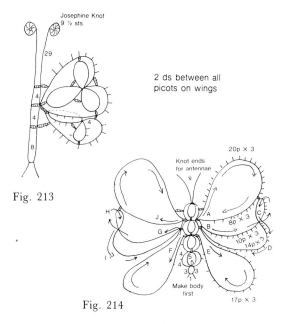

Fig. 213

Fig. 214

picots are the same on this side but have been omitted from the diagram so that the arrows could be clearly seen.

Make chain F in the direction of arrows and join into the body picot as shown. The next middle part is made in the same way as the first middle part—that is, not in reverse. This is so that the curve may be made properly. The top part of the wing, chain J, is made last and joined back into the picot between the head and the body. The ends are then cut and sewn in neatly.

This may appear to be complicated but if you take a little time to follow the arrows around the butterfly before you start, you will see that it really is quite simple.

Have fun with the butterflies and experiment with different types of thread including silver and gold for really special effects.

Tatted Doodles

We all doodle with a pen or pencil at odd moments so why not try doodling with your tatting shuttle in the same way?

These 'doodles' are all uncomplicated little items made with left-over scraps of cotton. When you were learning to tat you probably made odd rings which looked like rabbit's heads or funny-shaped dogs—well, that's all you do to make these doodles!

When chains are required, just unwind a length of thread from the shuttle before starting and this will save making joins with a ball of thread. On some of the doodles picots are cut to make legs, antennae, etc., and in some cases they have been cut and frayed with a pin to give a fluffy appearance.

Once you get the idea you'll see just how easy it is to doodle with a shuttle. Use the doodles to stick on party invitations for children and also place cards and gift tags. Add them to your tatted notepaper ideas.

Fig. 218.   Turtle

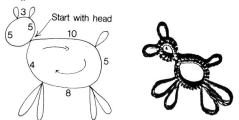

Fig. 215.   Dog

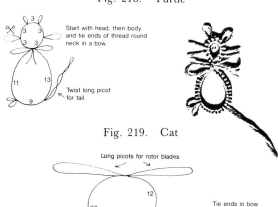

Fig. 219.   Cat

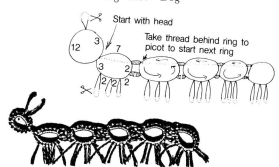

Fig. 216.   Caterpillar

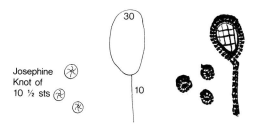

Fig. 217.   Tennis raquet and balls

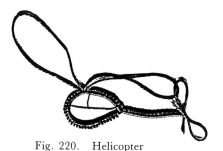

Fig. 220.   Helicopter

74

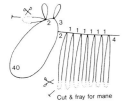

Fig. 221.   Horse

Start with head ring. Body is a chain.

10
2

RW

Tie end
of chain
between
2nd and
3rd double
stitch of 1st
chain.

9

18

Fig. 226.   Duck

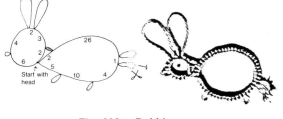

2 3
4   5
2
6   2   2
5
Start with
head

26

10   4

1

Fig. 222.   Rabbit

Start with head ring
Body is a chain tied
to the neck at the point
where the chain is reversed.

9
3

12

RW

35

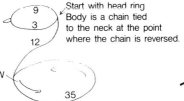

Fig. 227.   Swan

1
9
12
9   12
← Start

Fig. 223.   Fish

Don't RW
after head
ring.

4   6

10

20

22

2   2
Start with
body ring.

12

Tie into picot
to finish.

Fig. 228.   Snail

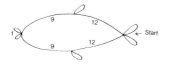

10
2   → Start with head

1

3

7

1
2
5

14

4

5

Long picot
twisted for tail

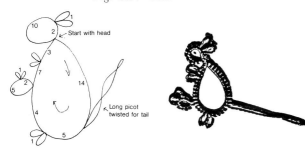

Fig. 224.   Kangaroo with Joey (2 shuttles). Head
is a ring. Body is a chain, Joey's head is a ring
worked with the second shuttle, then chain again
and tie at base of head to finish.

Join over eye ring picot leaving a
long loop in shuttle thread for beak

8

5
7
5

Long
loop for
beak

24

← Start with eye ring

Fig. 229.   Owl

Picots are cut close to
body and opened
out to become
long legs.

2   2   2

2   2

2   2

2   2

4   4

Start

Fig. 225.   Spider

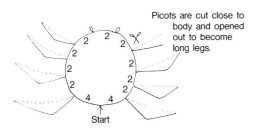

10   10

10   10

10   1 1 1   10

10

10

Start with ring, making 3 very long
picots with 2 short ones between
them. Twist long picots as chains are
joined into them.

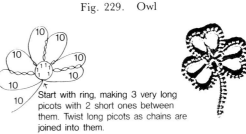

Fig. 230.   Shamrock

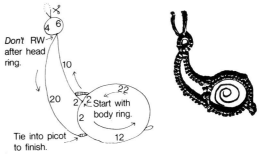

75

The zodiac doodles (figs 231–242) are a little more difficult than the ordinary ones, but with a little concentration and practice you will soon be able to make them just as easily.

Once you start, you will get plenty of your own ideas, but the main thing is to keep them simple.

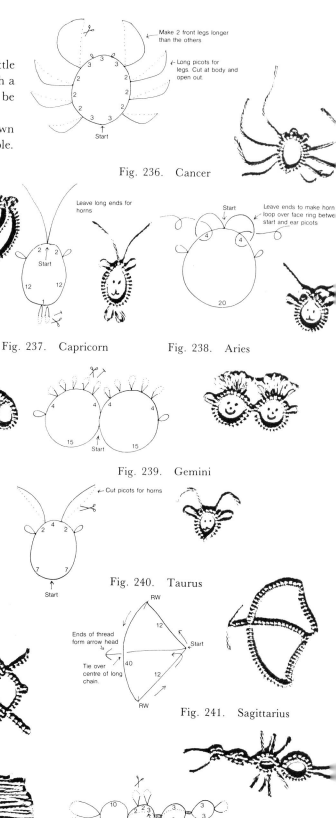

Make 2 front legs longer than the others

Long picots for legs. Cut at body and open out.

3 3
3 2
2 2
2 2
3 3
Start

Fig. 236.　Cancer

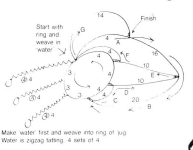

Start with ring and weave in 'water'

14　Finish
G
4　A
4　F
4　16
3　10
4　E
3　3
4　D
3　C　20
B

C 4
4
4

Make 'water' first and weave into ring of 'jug'.
Water is zigzag tatting. 4 sets of 4.

Fig. 231.　Aquarius

Leave long ends for horns

2 ↑ 2
Start
12　12
1

Fig. 237.　Capricorn

Start
Leave ends to make horn loop over face ring between start and ear picots

4　4

20

Fig. 238.　Aries

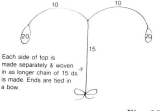

10　10
20　20
15

Each side of top is made separately & woven in as longer chain of 15 ds is made. Ends are tied in a bow.

Fig. 232.　Libra

4　4　4
15　15
Start

Fig. 239.　Gemini

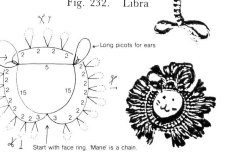

Long picots for ears

Join 'mane' in middle of ear picot by using shuttle thread.

2 2 2 2
2　2
5
2　2
15　15
2　2
2 2 2 2 2

Start with face ring. 'Mane' is a chain.

Fig. 233.　Leo

Cut picots for horns

2　4　2
7　7
Start

Fig. 240.　Taurus

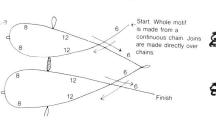

Start. Whole motif is made from a continuous chain. Joins are made directly over chains.

8　12
8　12　6
6
8　12　6 6
8　12　Finish

Fig. 234.　Pisces

RW
12
Ends of thread form arrow head
40　Start
Tie over centre of long chain.
12
RW

Fig. 241.　Sagittarius

6
10 long picots for hair
10
Start

76

Fig. 235.　Virgo

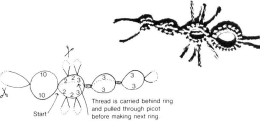

10　2 2 3　3　3
10　2 2 3　3　3
Start
Thread is carried behind ring and pulled through picot before making next ring.

Fig. 242.　Scorpio

Tatted Baskets

These little baskets are quick and easy to make and would look nice filled with tatted flowers. Make some to hold place cards at a wedding or party or fill with nuts or sweets.

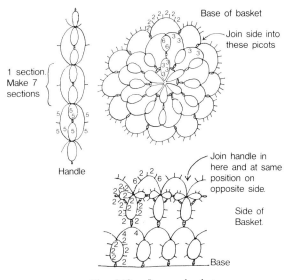

Fig. 243. Larger basket

With the larger of the two baskets (fig. 243) the base is made first and the ends are cut and finished neatly. The side of the basket is made next with the joins being made as explained in the introduction to 3-D tatting. It's a good idea to slip-stitch from the row which joins on to the base up to the row of cloverleafs. Do this after joining the end of the first row to the beginning to make a complete round.

After completing the cloverleaf row and making the last chain and joining it in the base of the first cloverleaf, *don't* cut the threads. Start making the handle with them, making sure the first ring of the handle comes as close as possible to the cloverleaf. This also applies with the second basket. After finishing the last row, the ball thread is cut and sewn in neatly and the shuttle alone is used to make the handle.

With the first basket the handle is made by working seven sections of the pattern, joining in the centre of a cloverleaf opposite the start of the handle, and then making the chain to match the other side all the way back to the beginning of the handle. Finish by cutting the threads and sewing in the ends.

The second basket is extremely quick and easy to make as the thread can be slip-stitched between each row (fig. 244).

After making the centre ring, the first two rows are just rings and chains, the third row is cloverleafs and chains and the final row starts

Tatted baskets. Stiffened, these make pretty table decorations for weddings or children's parties.

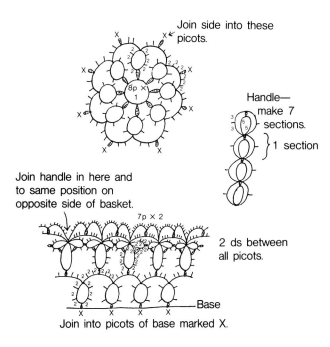

Join side into these picots.

Join handle in here and to same position on opposite side of basket.

Handle— make 7 sections.

} 1 section

2 ds between all picots.

7p × 2

Base

Join into picots of base marked X.

Fig. 244.   Smaller basket

where the third row finishes—in the centre of a cloverleaf, then that chain goes right around the edge of the basket, joining alternately into the middle picot of the chain of the last row and into the base of each cloverleaf.

When you get back to the beginning again and the last chain has been joined in, again, *don't* cut the thread to the shuttle, only the ball thread which is neatly sewn in.

With the shuttle make the first ring of the handle and then carry the thread behind the ring and up to the middle picot. Pull a loop through this and pass the shuttle through it and pull tight. Now make the next ring and so on until the required number has been made, then join the middle picot of the last ring into the base of a cloverleaf opposite the start of the handle. The thread is then cut and sewn in neatly.

By experimenting with different-sized threads you can make different-sized baskets for various purposes so try using various thicknesses of thread.

Tatted 3-D Flowers

We have seen earlier how to make the more usual kind of tatted flowers—flat ones which can be joined together to make borders or doilies, but here is something different—three-dimensional flowers which can be formed into tiny posies (figs 246–252).

These little posies can then be pinned to your dress for that special occasion or you can do as I do: mount them on black velvet in a picture frame and hang them on the wall. (Treat them with one of the dirt-repellant sprays available to protect them.)

Stamens for the flowers can be bought at most craft shops, as can the green plastic tape (non-sticky—the kind used for making artificial flowers). The stems are made from fine wire which is used to fix the stamens through the back of the flower. This wire is then covered with the green tape and the leaves are joined in as the tape is wound around the wire (fig. 245).

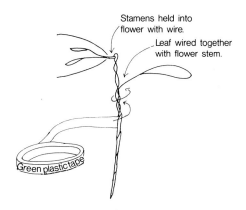

Fig. 245.   Joining in leaves and stamens

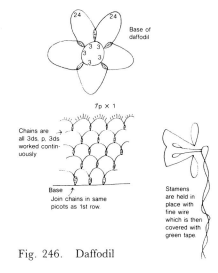

Fig. 246.   Daffodil

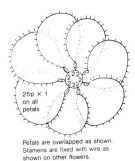

Petals are overlapped as shown. Stamens are fixed with wire as shown on other flowers.

Fig. 247.   Carnation

Flowers with a bell shape, such as the lilies of the valley, bluebells and even the trumpet of the daffodil are made continuously. That's to say, don't cut the thread each time you have completed a round or you will forever be joining in threads!

For the daisy and chrysanthemum make a ring with very long picots—about ten or twelve of them—and cut the ends so that you then have double the number of petals.

For a bulkier daisy make two identical rings and fix them together with the stamens. Try using a thick thread, too.

For the chrysanthemum make several rings with long picots and join them in the usual way. When stiffening them make sure the petals stand forward when drying.

Although the flowers will be fairly sturdy it is advisable to stiffen them as they will then stand up to much handling.

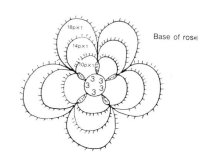

Base of rose

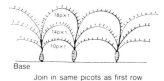

Base

Join in same picots as first row

Fig. 250. Rose

Cut ends

Fig. 251. Daisy and Chrysanthemum

Make centre ring and three inner chains black. Make outer chains in blues, purples or yellow.

Fig. 248. Pansy

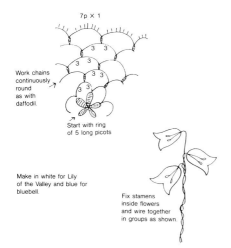

7p × 1

Work chains continuously round as with daffodil.

Start with ring of 5 long picots

Make in white for Lily of the Valley and blue for bluebell.

Fix stamens inside flowers and wire together in groups as shown.

Fig. 249. Lily of the Valley and Bluebell

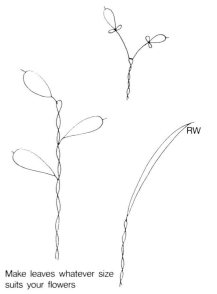

RW

Make leaves whatever size suits your flowers

Fig. 252. Leaves

A posy of tatted flowers mounted in a suitable frame can look very attractive.

Cover your Christmas tree with tatted decorations. Use different-sized thread to make various-size snowflakes.

Make a sample book to keep all those odds and ends where you've tried out different patterns. Use a small photo album with clear plastic pages.

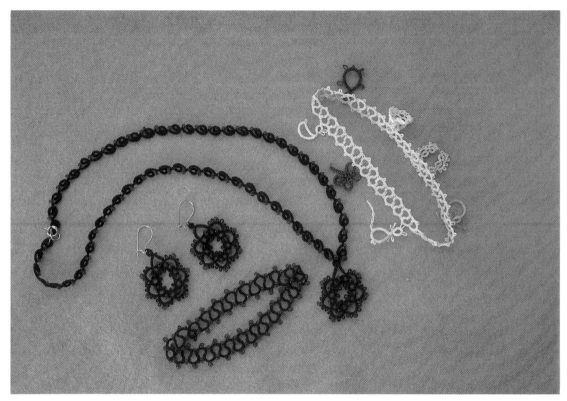

Tatted jewellery is unusual and very effective.

A tatted cap and belt made in wool using a netting needle instead of the usual shuttle.

Tatted Jewellery

Here's a chance to try your hand at beaded tatting—make some tatted jewellery! Here we have instructions for a charm bracelet (using your tatted doodles), and a necklace with matching earrings.

For the charm bracelet, the charms are made first. Select whichever doodles you want to use and make them with an extra picot on them so that they may be joined by it to the bracelet as it is being made (fig. 253).

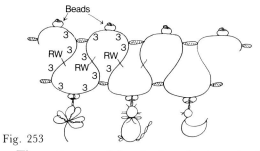

Fig. 253

The pattern used for the bracelet is a simple border which can be made with two shuttles or just one shuttle and a ball of thread. If you wish to put beads on the outer picots and you are using two shuttles, you will need to thread sufficient beads on to each shuttle before starting the bracelet. If you are using shuttle and ball, thread them on to the ball of thread before starting (fig. 254).

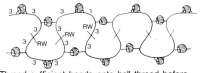

Thread sufficient beads onto ball thread before starting work (for top and bottom rows of beads). Beads between chains are slipped onto long picots before making joins.

Fig. 254.   Bracelet

If beads are to be placed on the picots which join the chains together instead of the outer rows there is no need to thread them on first. Just make the picots slightly longer and push the bead over each picot before making the joins.

The bracelet is joined as a complete circle, large enough to slip over the hand on to the wrist and thus does not need a fastening. However, if you wanted to, you could put one in.

For each earring, six beads are threaded on to the ball thread before starting. These are then pushed into position while making the chains. The beads between the rings are slipped over the long picots before joining to the next ring. Earring wires or studs may be bought at most craft shops (fig. 255).

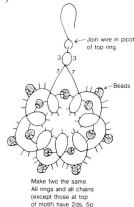

Make two the same.
All rings and all chains
(except those at top
of motif) have 2ds, 5p
× 2ds, 2ds

Fig. 255.   Earrings

For the matching necklace (fig. 256) you will need a clasp to fasten it—or you could use a hook and eye if you can't get a proper clasp.

Six beads need to be threaded on to the ball thread before starting. These are for the pendant, which matches the earrings.

The thread is looped through the clasp and one double stitch made to secure it before making the first ring of the necklace (fig. 256a). The beads are pushed over the long picots in the usual way and there are thirty beads between the clasp and the pendant in the centre of the necklace. This number can be adjusted to suit your requirements, but make sure it is the same number either side of the pendant.

The motif for the pendant is made in exactly the same way as the motif for the earrings. Once you have completed it make the other side of the necklace to match the first.

The sample shown was made with black thread and red beads, but choose any combination to suit yourself. The bracelet looks very special when made with a silver thread, but be sure to get a thread which is smooth to allow the stitches to slide. Your craft shop will be able to help you with this.

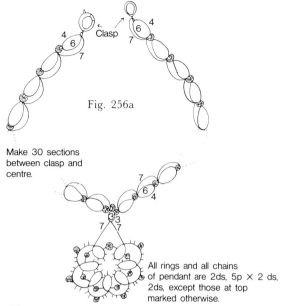

4
6
7
Clasp
4
6
7
Fig. 256a

Make 30 sections between clasp and centre.
7
6
4
3
3
7
7
All rings and all chains of pendant are 2ds, 5p × 2 ds, 2ds, except those at top marked otherwise.
Fig. 256

Christmas Tatting

A very obvious use for your tatting is to make tatted snowflakes for your Christmas tree (figs 257–262). Almost any motif can be adapted to look like a snowflake simply by making it in a fine white crochet cotton and making the picots slightly longer.

Stiffen snowflakes either with sugar and water solution or whatever method you prefer. (See chapter on handy hints for ways to stiffen tatting.) They may then be hung all around your Christmas tree, or even made into a special Christmas mobile. Make them in various sizes and add glitter dust for further interest.

You will probably wish to make quite a few

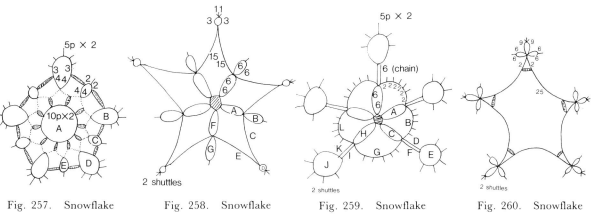

Fig. 257. Snowflake   Fig. 258. Snowflake   Fig. 259. Snowflake   Fig. 260. Snowflake

Fig. 261. Snowflake   Fig. 262. Snowflake

Tatted 3-dimensional bells.

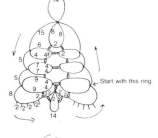

Fig. 263. Flat bell
(with clapper)

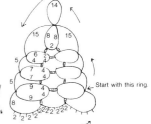

Fig. 264. Flat bell
(without clapper)

decorations for the festive season. I have designed only a small number of patterns, but by adding little bits here and there to the same pattern different items can be made. Thus you will only have to learn a couple of basic patterns to have a whole range of Christmas decorations.

The flat bell (figs 263, 264) can not only be hung from your tree, but can also be stuck on to your own personal Christmas cards! It is easier if it is made with two shuttles—top ring (handle) and bottom ring (clapper) both being made with the second shuttle.

By leaving out the clapper, adding a couple of wings and making the top ring larger for a head, you have a little angel (fig. 265).

Make four of these basic angel shapes, this time omitting the head and adding a few extra picots to join them together (fig. 266). Make

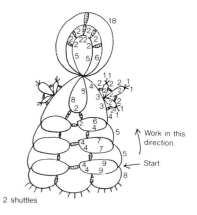

2 shuttles

Fig. 265. Angel from flat bell pattern

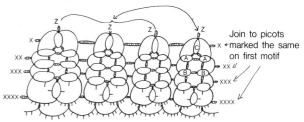

Make first 3 motifs in a line and join by top picot of last motif through top of picots of other 3 motifs

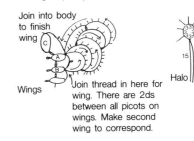

Join into body to finish wing

Wings

Join thread in here for wing. There are 2ds between all picots on wings. Make second wing to correspond.

A halo may be worked in between the wings if desired to avoid having to break off and rejoin thread. Slip-stitch from first wing to base of ring marked C on pattern. After making halo slip stitch to make second wing.

Halo

Three tatted angels—quick and easy to make.

Fig. 266. 3-D Angel

them in a strip and join the top picots (marked Z on the diagram) when you make the last one and before joining the first and last sides together. This makes it easier to handle whilst you are working.

Add a tiny polystyrene ball for a head (add face and hair too if you wish), some chains for wings, plus her star halo of course and you have a 3-D angel! A final row of chains around the bottom just adds a finishing touch!

A 3-D bell (fig. 267) can also be transformed

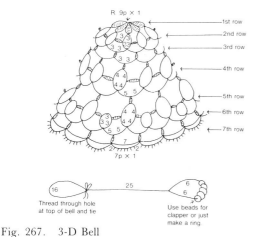

Fig. 267.   3-D Bell

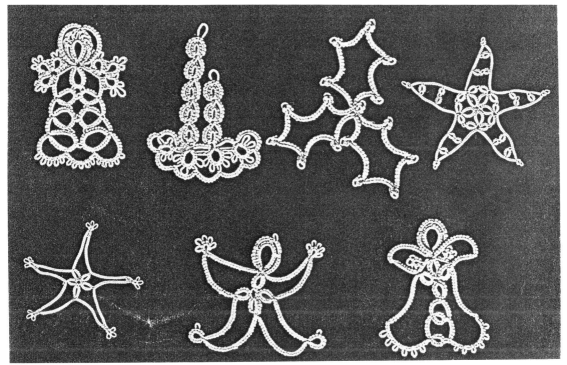

Wings

Fig. 268.   3-D Angel

into an angel by just adding wings and a polystyrene ball for the head (fig. 268). When making this bell (or angel) it is a good idea to slip stitch from one row to the next to avoid extra joins and also to speed up your work.

A smaller bell may be made by leaving out the fifth row (fig. 269).

These bells also look nice with beads added to

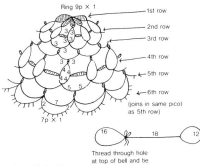

Fig. 269.   Small bell

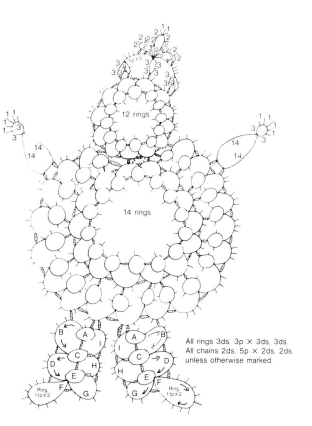

Fig. 271.   Santa Claus

All rings 3ds. 3p × 3ds. 3ds.
All chains 2ds. 5p × 2ds. 2ds.
unless otherwise marked.

the sixth row. Add pearl beads for a bride, and coloured beads for a new baby, and tie the bell to gifts.

How about a couple of candles to stick on to those personal cards you are making? If you are making the candles and wreath all the same colour, start with the taller candle, then the ring under it, chain to the short candle, then the ring below it and then clockwise until you are back at the base of the tall candle.

If you wish to make white candles and a red and green wreath, make the two candles separately and then the wreath, either weaving in the ends from the candles as you make the wreath or sewing them in afterwards (fig. 270).

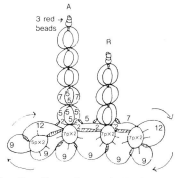

Fig. 270.   Candles and wreath. Make candle A first, then the ring below it. Next make the chain between candles, then candle B. Make wreath after this. If making candles a different colour, make both candles first and weave in ends while making wreath.

No Christmas is complete without Santa Claus and he is very easy to make in red and white with his black boots (fig. 271).

With white on your shuttle and red on the ball thread, make his head first and tie and cut the ends. Now make Santa's body using the same colour combination and joining to the head as

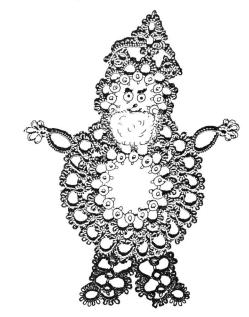

shown. Change to red shuttle and red ball and make the second row of Santa's body. With the same colours make his hat.

With a scrap of pink on the shuttle (use white

Tatted Santa Claus with a little Christmas clown, candles and wreath, and some holly leaves.

Tatted snowman and other tatted items to hang on your Christmas tree.

if you don't have pink, but it's not worth buying it specially) and red ball thread make his hands and join on as shown.

Lastly with black thread on both ball and shuttle make his boots.

A small circle of pink felt stuck in place will make a face with the addition of drawn or stuck-on eyes and a bit of cotton wool for a beard! And there's the jolliest Santa Claus ever!

Now make a snowman from the same basic pattern (fig. 272). Using white on both shuttle and ball thread this time make the same head and body as you did for Santa Claus. Make his hands in the same way too.

Using black thread (or whatever colour you prefer) for both shuttle and ball make his hat which is slightly different to Santa's. A scrap of bright red to make two rings which are tied in place to be his bow and you are almost finished.

In the pictures of snowmen we see on Christmas cards and in books they nearly always carry a stick and our pattern has one made from pearl tatting. If your memory needs refreshing, re-read the section on pearl tatting. However, if you cannot manage the pearl tatting try the alternative stick which is made from just rings.

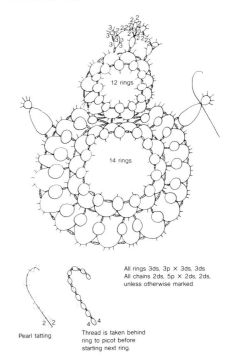

All rings 3ds, 3p × 3ds, 3ds
All chains 2ds, 5p × 2ds, 2ds, unless otherwise marked.

Pearl tatting

Thread is taken behind ring to picot before starting next ring.

Fig. 272. Snowman

Make lots of Santas and snowmen and hang them all over your Christmas tree. Hang some in the window too.

What about some holly leaves complete with

red berries? With dark green on both ball and shuttle they are very quickly made. To add the berries, just thread a couple of red beads on to the shuttle thread before winding it. If your shuttle and ball are still joined together, miss out the first tiny ring and make the first chain right up close to the beads. Then when the whole leaf is made, join the last chain to the base of the first chain, close to the beads. If your ball and shuttle are not joined, wind a length of thread from the shuttle, thread on the beads and use this length of thread instead of joining in a ball thread (fig. 273).

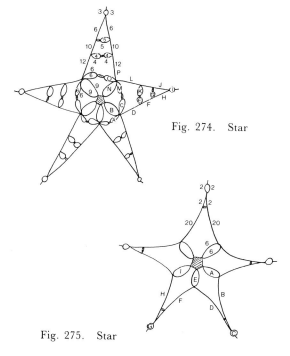

Fig. 273.   Holly

We mustn't forget to make a Christmas star. The two examples shown here (figs 274, 275) can be made in threads of various thicknesses to give different-sized stars.

Fig. 274.   Star

Fig. 275.   Star

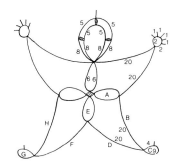

Fig. 276.   Small Santa or Clown

The smaller one (fig. 275) can easily be adapted to become a tiny Santa (fig. 276) if worked in red or even a clown, worked in any colour you like. (Add a tiny scrap of cotton wool for a beard if you're making a Santa.)

To make his hands and feet a different colour to the rings in the centre of the clown or Santa, start weaving in a short length of the colour required about six or so stitches before you need it. Then, when you come to the hand or foot, drop the shuttle and make the hand-ring or foot-ring with the other thread and after closing the ring, weave the other end of the thread back into the next chain for about six stitches. When the whole thing is finished, cut the protruding ends close to the chain (fig. 277).

Fig. 277.   Weaving in threads for Santa's hands

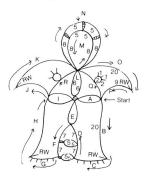

Fig. 278.   Angel 2 shuttles. Make outside of angel first and join bottom of second wing (O) to first ring, then do inner small chain (Q), join across neck, then do small chain R.

The angel (fig. 278) is worked by making the outside first and joining the bottom of the second wing (O) to the first ring. Now make the inner small chain (Q), join across the neck and make chain R.

These little figures could also be made in all kinds of colours for decorating children's clothes and party invitations.

Lastly, we have the Christmas Tree. Quite simply made, it is a triangle shape surrounded by another larger one. Then the trunk is made secondly, using brown instead of green (fig. 279).

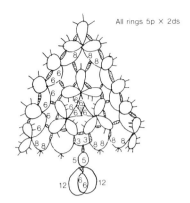

All rings 5p × 2ds

Fig. 279

The Tatting Bug

Be warned!! Once you have been bitten by this terrible creature your life will never be the same! There will be scraps of cotton all over the house, shuttles in every possible place. Meals will be forgotten, weeds will take over your garden and your family will be lucky to get a sensible word out of you!

Why? Because the penny has just dropped, all of a sudden your thread flicks over the right way and the only knots you are making are the ones you have been trying to make. You can tat at last!

Now that you have been bitten by the tatting bug you must make one to keep you company (fig. 280).

He is really very simple, being based on the traditional wheel motif. You will need some fine wire—the covered kind used for making artifical flowers is good, or even a piece of fuse wire (the 15 amp size). This is to make his legs and feelers. Also some small plastic eyes (from a craft shop) to be stuck on to the ends of the feelers.

The main body of rings is made first and then as you make the outside chain the wire is

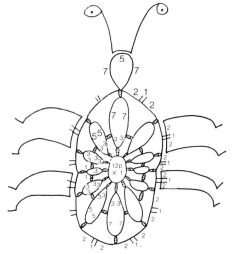

Fig. 280. The Tatting Bug. Make chains over wire, and head ring over wire for feelers.

threaded through the stitch in the same way as when weaving in loose ends. In other words, the stitch is made over the wire to conceal it and hold it in place.

When the whole bug is finished the legs are bent into shape and the plastic eyes are stuck on.

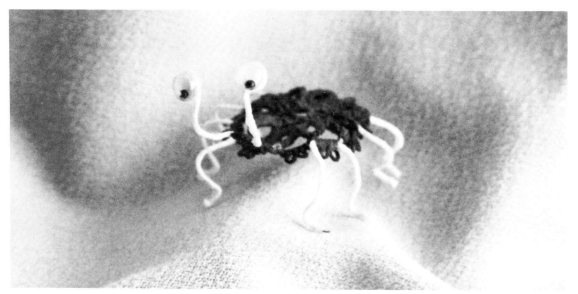

The Tatting Bug! Beware, once he has bitten you become a tattoholic!

Tatted Alphabet and Numbers

There are several tatted alphabets available in various books on tatting, the most popular, perhaps, being the one in the Julia Sanders book published by Dover Books.

The alphabet given here is not as elaborate as that one, as sometimes you need only a plain initial to put on your tatted notepaper or in the corner of a hankie (fig. 281).

To save joins, if your shuttle is not attached to the ball of thread just pull a metre or so of thread from the shuttle and use it as the ball.

All the letters start with a ring of five picots with one double stitch between. This gives you something to hold on to while you are making the letter. They mostly finish with a ring of three picots.

Since the letter will be stuck on to something such as notepaper or a hankie, the back of it will not be seen and as it will have some sort of glue on it, any threads should not come undone. Therefore, when you come to the last little ring of each letter, cut the ball thread off, leaving about five centimetres. Weave this thread into the last ring as you make it and when the letter is made cut both threads (shuttle and the end of the ball thread). This will avoid sewing in ends and also a knot which could be bumpy when the letter is stuck down.

In letters which have loops—such as B, C, J— the joins are made over the chain and not by picots.

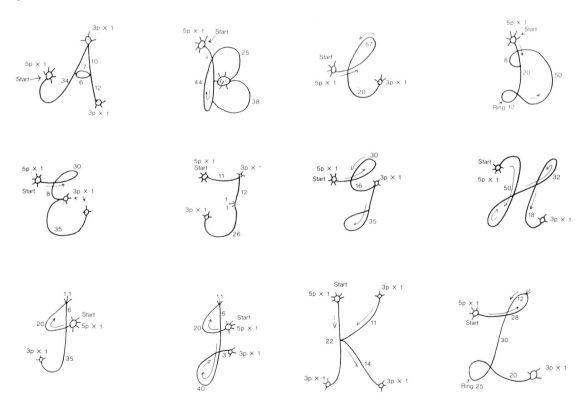

Fig. 281

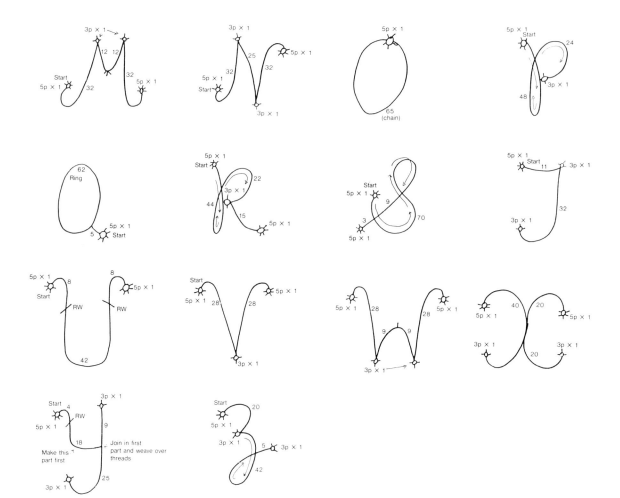

Fig. 281 contd.

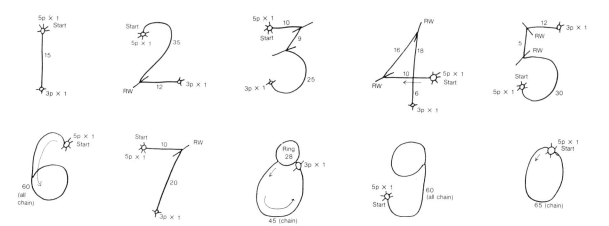

Fig. 282

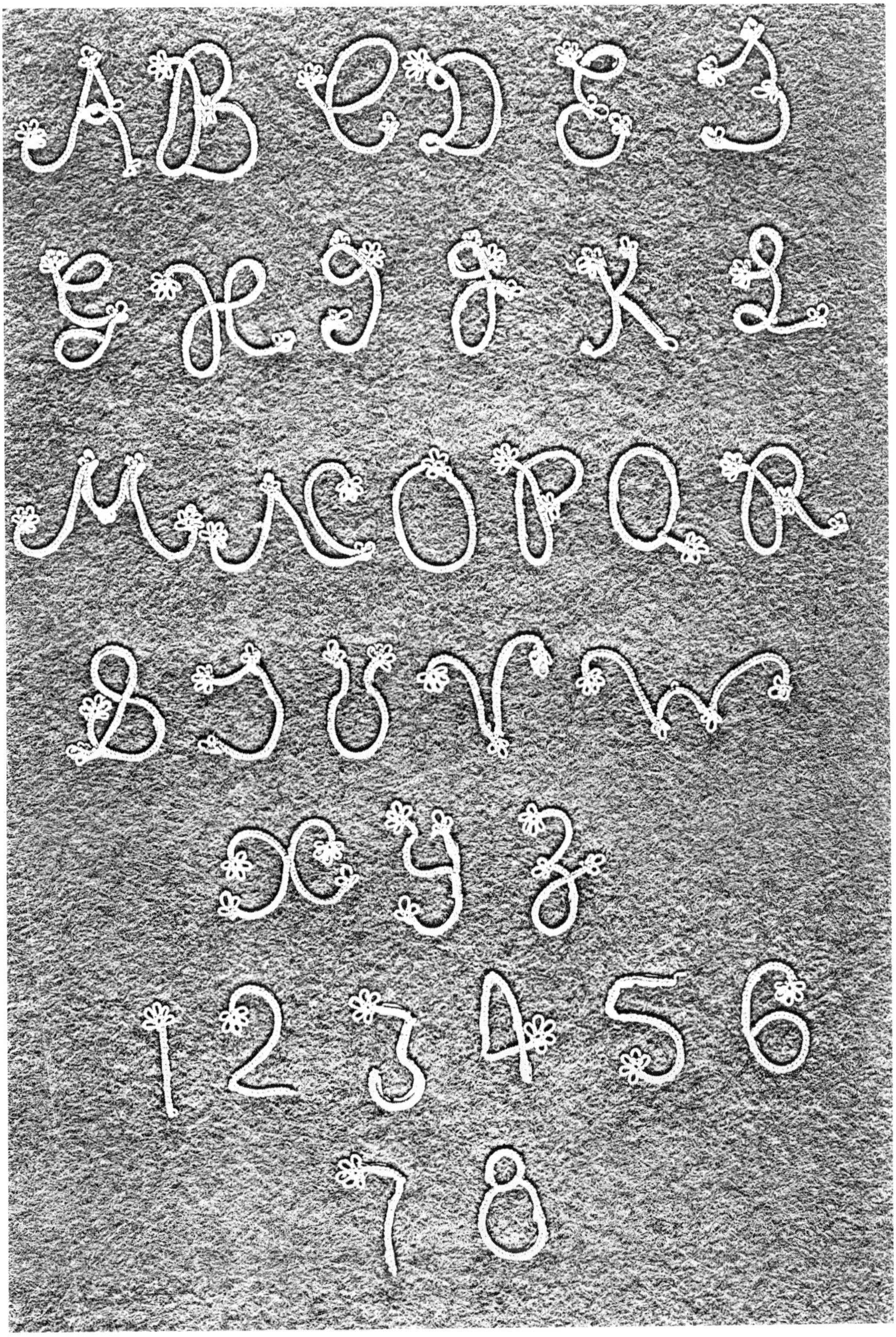

Tatting for Babies

What could be lovelier than seeing a pretty baby dressed in a dainty tatted bonnet and bootees! Not very practical items of clothing, I will admit, but guaranteed to bring forth a chorus of oohs and aahs from non-tatters!

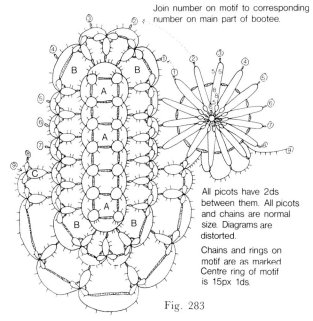

Join number on motif to corresponding number on main part of bootee.

All picots have 2ds between them. All picots and chains are normal size. Diagrams are distorted.

Chains and rings on motif are as marked. Centre ring of motif is 15px 1ds.

Fig. 283

Worked in a no. 40 to 50 crochet cotton the bootees will have approximately a 7.5 cm sole. To vary the size, use a larger or smaller size thread (fig. 283).

Start with the sole of the bootee, making the round of rings and chains first (A on the pattern). Either tie and cut your threads or slip-stitch to the next row of cloverleafs and chains which joins to the first row (marked B).

The threads are cut after this row and the flower motif is made next, starting with a ring of fifteen picots with one double stitch between them. The petals of this flower motif are joined to the chain of the cloverleaf row as shown in the diagram (count five chains down from the centre

A tatted baby's bootee turned into a pin-cushion by filling the inside with black velvet.

cloverleaf at the end of the sole) and the ends are then tied and cut.

The final row starts with a cloverleaf (C) on the chain next to the motif and the small ring of the new cloverleaf nearest the motif joins to the nearest petal (8 in the diagram). Continue this row round the end of the bootee until you reach the flower motif at the other side and join in to match the beginning.

Continue the chain around the flower as shown and finish it back at the first cloverleaf of this row at the point marked 9 on the diagram.

Thread a ribbon through the chain of the last row and tie in a bow.

The bonnet (fig. 284) is particularly easy to make as it is made flat and gathered into shape by a ribbon at the back.

Made with size 10 crochet cotton our bonnet had nine flowers in the bottom row, but you may vary according to the size you want and the thread you are using. Remember to adjust the other rows to match. Make the picots in the centre petals of the bottom row of flowers long enough to thread your ribbon through. This is then gathered into a circle and tied to give shape to the bonnet. Ribbons are also sewn to the last flower at each end of the third row (the long row) to tie under baby's chin.

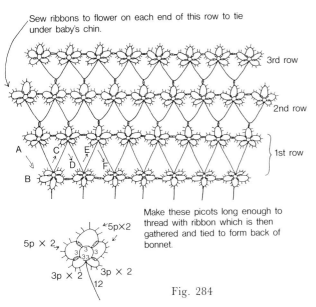

Sew ribbons to flower on each end of this row to tie under baby's chin.

3rd row

2nd row

1st row

A
B
C
D
E
F

5p × 2
5p×2
5p × 2
3p × 2
3p × 2
12

Make these picots long enough to thread with ribbon which is then gathered and tied to form back of bonnet.

Fig. 284

Make the bonnet and bootees as a special gift for a new mother. Even if you don't know anyone with a baby, you can still find a good excuse to make the bootees—or at least one of them.

Make just one bootee and then using a scrap of dark velvet, make a padded insertion to go inside the bootee—big enough to fill it and give it shape. You now have a unique pin-cushion!

With the growing interest in facsimile antique dolls these days, tatting is an obvious choice when dressing them. Make borders and motifs to trim their old-fashioned dresses. Use the finest thread available—no. 100 or 80 is best. As these sizes are hard to get in any colour other than white, after making your lace, dip it in a solution of coffee or tea to achieve the creamy ecru colour that was so popular in Victorian times.

Tatted Cats

If, like me, you are very fond of cats, you will enjoy making these two tatted cats.

They are quite easy and can be made in any colour combination to match your own favourite feline.

For the sitting cat make the ears first, then the head, joining in the ears as you go. Then make the body and join the head on to it (fig. 285).

The running cat has the same head and ears as the sitting cat and these are made first. Next make the five-ring motif in the middle of his tummy. Now the body, legs and tail are made, joining to the other parts as you go (fig. 286).

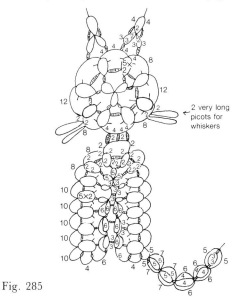

2 very long picots for whiskers

Fig. 285

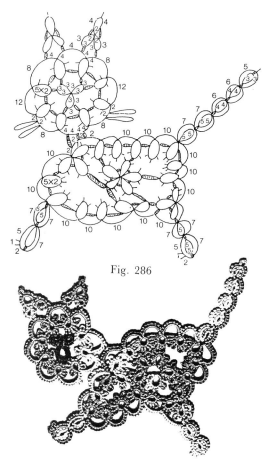

Fig. 286

The eyes and nose of both cats were worked in different colours using needle tatting, but they can be made in one three-ring piece with ordinary tatting and joined into the head as you go.

If you use a varigated yellow you can make a lovely ginger cat, or, using brown and cream, make my favourite—the Siamese.

General Hints to Make Tatting Easier

As with most things, there are often short cuts in tatting which will make your work both faster and easier. Some will seem pretty obvious once you have read them; others you may need to practise at first, but will save a lot of time in the long run. Other hints are aimed at the lazy tatter (and there are lots of us, let's admit it!) who doesn't want to be sewing in ends every five minutes. From experience, I know that it's little things like this that put a lot of people off tatting. So read all the hints, try them, and you'll find that tatting can be lots of fun without lots of extra and unnecessary work!

If possible, always start your tatting with a ring. This makes it much easier to weave in your threads, as a ring gives you something to hold on to at the beginning of work. Also, if you are running out of thread during the course of work, arrange it so that you start the new thread with a ring. ———

It's a good idea to have an extra ball of thread, the same colour as that which you are using, handy when working a piece of tatting which you know will require more than one shuttleful of thread. That way, you will not need to cut the ball thread to rewind the shuttle and will thus only have one new thread to weave in. If you don't have the extra ball of thread, wind two or more shuttles before starting to tat, but remember not to cut the last shuttle that you wind from the ball. This way you will avoid that first join.

When using two colours, rings are the colour of the shuttle thread and chains are the colour of the ball thread. To get rings of two colours or chains of two colours, two shuttles must be used. To do this, one shuttle is used as the ball thread until rings of that colour are required and then the first shuttle is dropped and the second shuttle is used as the shuttle. If chains of the colour of

the first shuttle are needed, it must be used as the ball thread and the second shuttle used as the shuttle.

It's a good idea to let the shuttle hang down free every now and then to let the thread untwist. This is particularly so if you are making something using tatted rings only.

Be sure to always reverse your work after making a ring and before starting a chain and vice versa, unless the pattern states otherwise. Then make your first double stitch of the new ring or chain as close as possible to the previous work to avoid gaps.

Where it can be done conveniently it is a good idea (saving time by having less ends to sew in) to slip stitch from one row to the next. To do this, after finishing the first row, do not cut the threads to start the next row. Leave a space along the threads of both shuttle and ball sufficient to carry you to the place where the first ring of the next row will be and then make the ring. This will mean that there will be loose threads behind the work (thus making a 'back' and a 'front' of the work which doesn't usually happen in tatting). These threads can be oversewn to the back of the finished piece of tatting if desired but it isn't really necessary. Naturally it is also possible to slip stitch if using a shuttle only. Be sure to allow enough thread between rows so that your work does not get pulled out of shape (fig. 287).

Fig. 287

When winding a shuttle do not overfill it by having the thread outside the blades. This will not only slow you down, but it may cause the blades to be forced apart at the tips, which will let the thread unravel if the shuttle is hanging loose. Also, if using a white or light-coloured thread it could get dirty from too much handling.

When pressing tatting, always iron it under a damp cloth with the right side of the work (if there is one) face down. Always wash by hand and roll in a towel to remove surplus moisture. Lay flat on a towel to dry and if necessary pin out the picots after pulling gently into shape.

To wash something like a collar, first wrap some cloth (a piece of old sheet, etc.) around a large bottle such as a lemonade bottle and fasten it by either oversewing or tying. Place the tatting around this, keeping it in its proper shape with all picots flat and in place. Finally cover the tatting with another piece of old sheet or cloth to keep it in place and fasten it so that it won't come off during washing (fig. 288). Dip the whole

Fig. 288

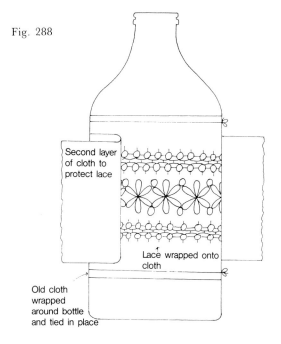

Second layer of cloth to protect lace

Lace wrapped onto cloth

Old cloth wrapped around bottle and tied in place

thing in washing suds and swish it about until you think the tatting will be clean, then rinse it thoroughly, still on the bottle.

Once rinsed the top covering may be removed and the tatting (still on the bottle) rolled in a towel to absorb any wetness. Finally, remove the tatting carefully and lay flat on a towel to dry. It should be still in the right shape and should not need pinning out.

To stiffen tatting such as the 3-D bells and baskets, or even doilies, dip into a solution of two cups of sugar dissolved in one cup of water and allowed to cool. Dab off any excess liquid with tissue or kitchen paper after soaking the item thoroughly. Stretch into shape and allow to dry. The solution may be kept in a screw-top jar and re-used.

PVA glue, which is white but dries clear, is quite good for stiffening, but a bit messy to apply. If you don't have any rubber gloves, put a large plastic bag over each hand before starting. Squeeze the glue onto the item to be stiffened and work it into the stitches with your fingers (inside the gloves or bags). Poke through any picots which have filled up with the glue with a toothpick and then pull the items into shape. Leave in a warm place to dry, checking that they have kept their shape every so often.

Another method is to use two envelopes of gelatine dissolved in boiling water; add a table-spoon of epsom salts. Stir until dissolved and add sufficient cold water to completely immerse article. Leave soaking for a few minutes and then pull into shape and allow to dry in a warm spot.

To stiffen something tatted in very fine thread such as small snowflakes, you can spray them with hair spray. Wait until they are dry and spray again if they are not stiff enough.

Strictly speaking, tatting should look the same on both sides—that is, there should be no actual front or back to the work. However, to be practical, you should decide which is to be the front or the back so that all your finishing off may be done on the one side.

Once you have decided, mark the wrong side or back by tying a thread of a different colour loosely through the work and knot the ends, then make all knots (hopefully there shouldn't be any!) and joins of loose ends on that side. If you do have joining knots, leave all ends until the work is finished and then sew in neatly with one thread taken to the right and one to the left before cutting the loose ends. It's better to do this when the work is finished as there will be no more strain on the threads from being worked and thus less chance of coming undone.

One of the most common problems encountered when tatting is what to do about hands which keep getting hot and sticky and so make the tatting look grubby. Some people do have hands which get sweaty very easily and no matter how many times they are washed and dried, the problem remains.

The best thing is to rub a little talcum powder into your hands before you start work and each time you feel your hands beginning to get a bit damp, rub in a little more.

A friend of mine who likes to tat in the train on the way to work each morning keeps her talcum in a tiny pill box which she tucks into her tatting bag, thus it is always handy without taking up the space that an ordinary tin of talcum would.

Someone also suggested to me that plain white cotton gloves could be worn whilst tatting, but I think they would slow the work down a great deal.

If, for some reason or other, the blades of your shuttle have become too wide apart at the tips, sometimes there is a solution. If the shuttle is made of plastic you can soak it in quite warm water for a minute or two and then put spring-type clothes pegs over the ends of the blades for a short time (fig. 289). Do not leave them on for too long as it could damage the blades.

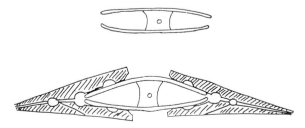

Fig. 289

This method can also be used on tortoiseshell shuttles *if you are very careful*, but don't have the soaking water much more than warm. I wouldn't advise doing it to bone or ivory shuttles unless the post in between the blades is quite small and will not cause the blades to be forced together. *Never*, repeat, *never* try to change the blades of an antique shuttle or you may ruin it forever.

Here is a hint which I was told to be sure to include by a physiotherapist friend I taught to tat. When you are concentrating on your tatting, particularly when you are learning, many people, without being aware of it, tend to hunch up their shoulders and their body becomes quite tense. After a time, when you stop, you realise that your neck is stiff and there is a burning pain across your shoulders. If you feel yourself hunching up, just relax, drop your shoulders and rest for a minute, then when you start again, try to stay relaxed. When you know about it and can look for it, this pain can often be avoided.

Another medical problem which can arise from too much tatting is what is commonly called tennis elbow. Because of the way we sit when tatting with the arms bent and the movement of the wrist, certain muscles are used more than they are normally and if you do an excessive amount of tatting it can cause quite a bit of pain. The reason I include this information (which could possibly put you off tatting) in a book which is trying to promote the art, is that it may just help to make your tatting more comfortable. I speak from personal experience. One Christmas I had heaps of tatting to do—presents, decorations, etc., and some demonstration pieces which were needed in a hurry—and just sat tatting morning, noon and night for days on end. I paid dearly for it by not being allowed to use my right arm (on orders from the physiotherapist) for the whole of January, plus having to do lots of fiddly exercises. My case was very extreme, but I tell it as a warning not to overdo it. With normal tatting, it should not occur.

It is a good idea to make a sample book. Work a few centimetres of a favourite edging, some different motifs you've found and stick them into a small notebook complete with directions and notes as to what size thread you have used in your sample. Alternatively, put them into one of those small photo albums which you can buy at most chain stores quite cheaply. You don't have to copy out pages and pages of directions—make a diagram pattern such as the ones shown in this book and slide it into the album next to your sample. This will not only save you time when next you want to make that pattern, but you have a worked example right next to it.

In Victorian times, to help them make their picots, ladies used a ring-and-pin. This was a little gilt pin fixed to a small ring by means of a short chain. They put the ring over their left thumb and then as they needed to make a picot, they just flicked the pin up into place, made their picot and dropped the pin again.

These days, we make our picots without pins, but sometimes if the shuttle has no hook or point on the end, we still need help when joining picots, and have to use a small crochet hook.

Therefore, what I do is fix a small chain to one of the tiny hooks which come with the Milwards shuttle. The other end of the chain is fixed to a large safety pin which is then pinned to my blouse whilst I'm tatting. I find this more convenient than having it dangling from my thumb (fig. 290).

I also have my stitch unpicker (yes—I still have to unpick occasionally!) hanging by a chain from the same pin. If you had a pair of folding scissors you might even have them on the pin too.

If you don't have one of the Milwards mini-hooks, you can make your own by cutting the hook about three centimetres down from a fine crochet hook (use a hacksaw). Cut a small piece of fine dowel (only about five centimetres long) and make a hole in the centre of one end, fill it with a strong adhesive and push the cut end of the crochet hook into it.

Let it set and then drill a small hole in the other end to take the chain (fig. 291).

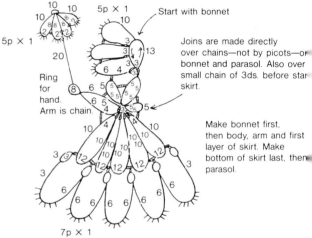

Fig. 292. Lady with a parasol

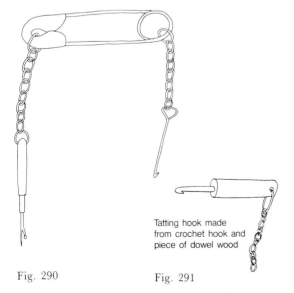

Tatting hook made from crochet hook and piece of dowel wood

Fig. 290   Fig. 291

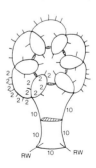

Fig. 293. Tree. 2 shuttles. This is just a suggestion—size may be varied by adding more rings to top of tree and lengthening trunk. Make it using 2 colours.

By mounting small motifs such as the two colonial ladies (figs. 292, 294) in appropriate frames, you can make some pretty little pictures.

Did you ever think of making pictures from your little tatted motifs? Cut a piece of felt to a bowl like shape and stick it on to a piece of cardboard. Now add tatted flower motifs worked in different colours. Add some butterflies too. Put it in a frame and you have an original picture!

Try a crinoline lady with her parasol, standing under a shady tree (figs 292, 293) or the lady without the parasol (fig 294) as she is very easy

to make (there is no sewing-in of ends). Give her a little dog (from the doodles section).

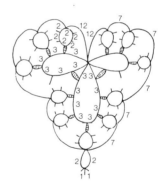

Fig. 295.   Heart motif

Fig. 296.   Netting Needle. They come in various sizes. Don't pull ring thread too tight when tatting with wool.

If you wish to tat something using wool or even a thick knitting cotton, obviously you will not get very much onto a shuttle. Try using a netting needle, which can be bought at most craft shops (fig. 296). Use it in the same way that you use your shuttle and make a woollen Juliet cap as

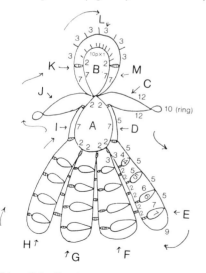

Fig. 294.   Crinoline lady motif. Tie ends round neck after working M to form bow for bonnet. (Lady is made all in one piece with absolutely no ends to sew in!)

Julet cap tatted in 8-ply wool. A netting needle is used instead of a shuttle when tatting with wool.

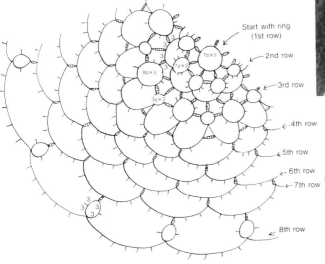

Fig. 297.   Juliet cap.

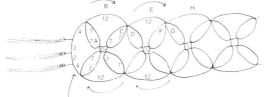

Work along one side first for length required, each end is the same as below, then along the other side

This chain is made last. Thread long strands through the picots to fasten belt.

Fig. 298.   Tatted belt

Cap and jacket tatted in 8-ply wool. The jacket is made by joining motifs together and the pattern for the cap is shown in fig. 297.

shown in fig. 297 and a belt to match (fig. 298) using two colours—the ring colour on your netting needle (shuttle) and a contrasting colour as your ball of thread.

When making items which won't have to be washed such as tatted snowflakes, motifs for mobiles, or even earrings and jewellery, you can avoid tedious sewing-in of ends by making a knot in the final ends, cutting them off quite close to the work and then adding a dab of PVA glue to the knot. This will prevent any accidental undoing. The PVA glue goes on white but dries clear and so will not be noticed on the finished article. Use the glue also for the small pieces you put into your sample book.

Remember, tatting is fun and you can do anything you like with it!

Mlle Riego and Tatting in Victorian Times

Victorian ladies were very interested in all forms of needlework, and tatting, while not as popular as crochet perhaps, had quite a large following.

This was mainly due to the remarkable Mlle Eleonore Riego de la Branchardiere.

Mlle Riego (as she was always known) was born in England of an Irish mother and a French father. Her father had escaped to England after the French revolution, so possibly he was from a noble family.

There is not much early information on Riego other than the fact that she had a 'fancy warehouse' in New Bond Street, London, in 1850, and this supplied lace-making and embroidery materials.

She must have been an excellent all-round needlewoman for she was appointed Artiste in Needlework to the Princess of Wales (later Queen Alexandra) and she won prizes at the Great Exhibition in 1851 and also in 1855 and 1862 for tape-based lace or Modern Point Work as it was called.

Mlle Riego wrote instruction booklets on crochet as well as those on tatting and they sold for between sixpence and one shilling at the time. In one of Riego's booklets she advertises her New Tatting Case which sounds just the thing every tatter would have wanted. 'Designed expressly to contain Book of Instructions, Cottons and every requisite for the work. It is made in Russian Leather and forms an elegant little work-box for presents, etc. Price 12 shillings and 6 pence'.

Wouldn't it be wonderful to find one somewhere in an antique shop!

Now on to Riego's method of tatting. I have included it in this book as I think it will be of great interest to anyone curious about early tatting and its history.

As explained in the instructions given for the first method of tatting in the chapter on how to tat, tatters in Riego's time worked the second half of the stitch first and what we call the first half of the stitch second. In those days what we now call the second half was called the English stitch and our present first half was called the French stitch.

Here are Riego's directions. The illustrations which accompany the instructions have been copied from her's.

Fill the shuttle with cotton or silk required and hold it in the right hand. Take the thread between the thumb and forefinger of the left hand, letting the end fall into the palm. Then with the right hand pass the thread from the shuttle around the other fingers of the left hand loosely, bringing it back to the thumb and forefinger and hold the threads quite tight, keeping the right hand lower than the left as shown in the drawing (fig. 299).

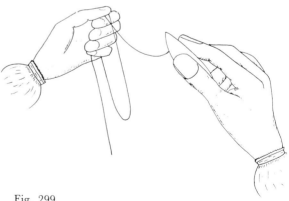

Fig. 299

Raise the second finger of the left hand so as to loosen the loop. Pass the shuttle through the back part of the loop, bringing it in front between the two threads (fig. 300) and holding the foundation (shuttle) thread quite tight, raise the right hand above the left. The foundation thread

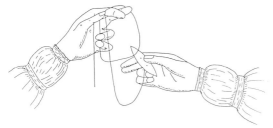

Fig. 300

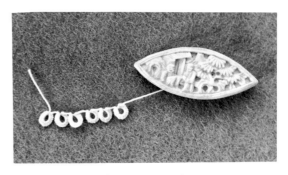

Riego's edging of loops made of 20 single stitches. The shuttle is of carved ivory (1800).

will now divide the loop into two parts, and still holding the foundation thread quite tight, remove the second finger from the upper part of the loop, and, placing it in the lower part, raise it up, so as to draw the upper part of the loop tight, which places it between the finger and thumb, and finishes the stitch. The stitches being formed by the loop round the fingers, the foundation thread should be capable of contracting or expanding the loop.

Riego's instructions then tell how to make an edging using 'ovals' by this method, telling us to commence a loop and work 20 single stitches as directed, withdraw the fingers from the loop, and draw the foundation thread tight. Commence the next oval close to the one already worked. If you make this pattern you will see that what you have made is actually an edging of what we now call Josephine knots, only slightly larger with a more open centre, because Josephine knots usually have less stitches.

To form the reverse or French stitch which turns the single stitch into the double knot of tatting Mlle Riego tells us to commence a loop and work a single stitch. Then raise the second finger, pass the foundation (shuttle) thread under it towards the back of the left hand, lowering the right hand. Bring the shuttle in front and pass it through the loop between the two threads that are nearest the right hand. Place the second finger in the lower part of the loop and draw it tight as in the single stitch (fig. 301).

You will notice that the stitch you have just made looks like the back of modern double stitch. Compare them—in fig 302 (a) is the modern double stitch looking at it as you have just made it and (b) is Riego's stitch as you have just made it. Fig. 303 shows one complete stitch and the

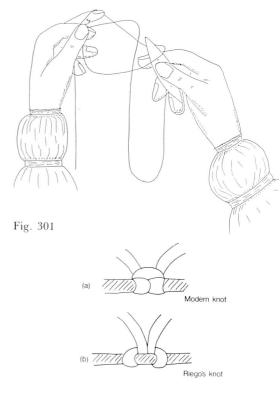

Fig. 301

(a)   Modern knot

(b)   Riego's knot

Fig. 302

Fig. 303

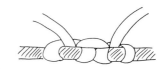

Fig. 304

first half of the next one. Fig. 304 shows two complete stitches, so you can see that they look quite different from modern-day tatting.

Making a picot was also quite a different affair.

Picots were called Purls or Pearls and a special purling pin or mesh was used. This was a gilt pin attached to a small ring by a chain (fig. 305). The

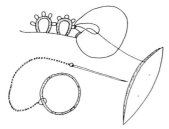

Fig. 305. Riego's 'New Method of Joining' using the ring and pin

ring was slipped over the thumb of the left hand and the pin hung down until it was needed. After making the required number of stitches, the thread around the hand was twisted around the pin, which was now being held by the thumb and forefinger, and then the double stitches were continued. When the pin was removed a loop had been formed. The pin was then dropped until needed again. One advantage to this method was that all your picots were even (figs 306–309).

Fig. 306. The ring thread is twisted round the pin

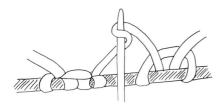

Fig. 307. The next stitch is made after twisting thread around the pin

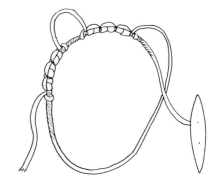

Fig. 308. The pin is removed and the picot is formed

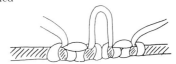

Fig. 309. The finished picot in place

The earliest method of joining tatting together was to tie each section and so build up your piece of work. Joining picots together during the actual working of the tatting was done with a needle instead of a shuttle. This was done by passing a needle through the picot of the piece you are joining to, then holding the picot between the thumb and forefinger and continuing with the ring, taking care that the foundation thread will still draw through the stitches (figs 310, 311).

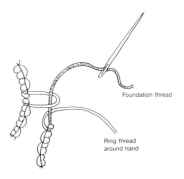

Fig. 310. Passing foundation thread through picot to join

Chains as we know them today were not invented until about 1864 and prior to this all tatting was done with a shuttle (or needle) only.

To make the work sturdier and less fragile, the threads between rings were often crocheted over

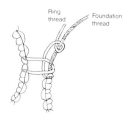

Ring thread   Foundation thread

Fig. 311. First half of next stitch being made after the join

Crochet 3 chains between each picot for heading

Fig. 313. Riego's oeillet edging

after the tatting was finished, and almost all tatted edgings had a crocheted heading with which to join it to whatever it had been made for.

Sometimes, instead of crocheting over the thread, a buttonhole stitch was worked with a

needle which was threaded with the cotton or silk from the shuttle (and left attached) before the tatting was started (fig. 312).

These buttonholed threads were called bars and in some old patterns chains are referred to as bars. Once tatted chains had been invented they were sometimes called long tatting and the rings were called round tatting.

A simple edging of half-closed tatted rings. A crocheted heading is worked after the tatting is completed (bone shuttle and crochet hook).

Fig. 312. A sewing needle is threaded to the shuttle thread before starting so that buttonhole stitches can be made over the spaces between rings

Riego used several different names for rings in her patterns. A row of rings by themselves were circles; small rings were oeillets or eyelets and larger ones were called ovals; sets of three rings in a cloverleaf formation were called trefoils. Later, the small rings were called dots and this name was used until around the turn of the century.

It's interesting to note that when Riego gave instructions for making a tatted chain—she called it a straight thread—she suggests using two shuttles, as well as a shuttle and ball of thread or a shuttle and a needle.

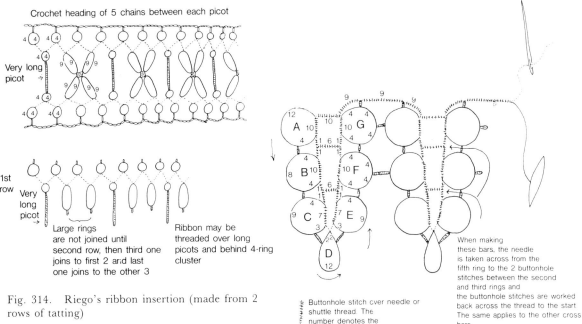

Fig. 314. Riego's ribbon insertion (made from 2 rows of tatting)

Fig. 315. Edging with buttonholed bars

I have included some of the old patterns of Riego and her contemporaries in case you would like to try them (figs 313–315). Of course, you could bring them right up to date by making modern chains instead of the crocheted or buttonholed bars if you prefer, but I like to make them in their original form.

Riego's œillet edging. The tatting is done with shuttle only and the threads between the rings are crocheted over afterwards. The shuttle is treen (1870) and the crochet hook is a late-Victorian steel hook.

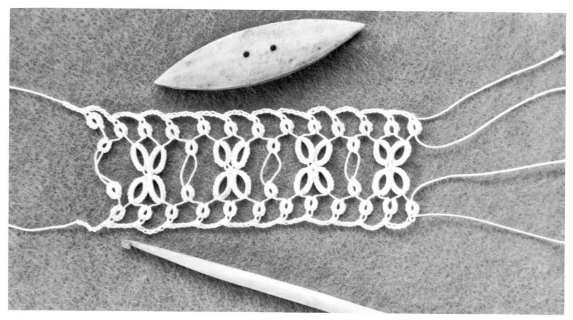

Ribbon insertion from one of Riego's books. A ribbon may be threaded behind the groups of four rings. The headings are crocheted over single threads. Shuttle is handmade from whalebone (1860) and the crochet hook is bone (1860).

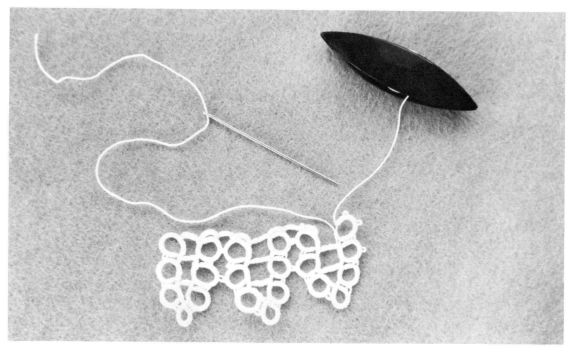

Vandyke border with buttonholed bars between the rings. Here the rings are only partially closed and buttonhole stitch is worked over the gaps as the work progresses. It is also worked over the threads between the rings during the making of the lace. Shuttle is tortoiseshell (1880).

Tatting from European Patterns

One day, while taking a tatting class, one of the students came up to me with a pattern she had found of a rather complicated doily. The illustration was quite clear but the instructions were in German. Unfortunately no one in the class spoke German, so we set about trying to work out the pattern by following the photograph and picking out numbers here and there throughout the pattern and checking them off on the photo of the doily.

Eventually, with the translation of some very easy words such as *doppelknotten* which obviously meant double knot and *pikot* which had to be picot, between us we managed to work out sufficient directions for the doily to be made.

Some European magazines publish tatting patterns in the diagram form used throughout this book, so naturally anyone, anywhere, can follow them. The same goes for Japanese patterns, but if you find a written pattern you wish to make, it's infuriating not to be able to follow it as easily as you might had it been written in English.

So, to help all those who have foreign patterns put aside waiting until you happen to meet a French, German, Italian or Spanish speaking person who will translate for you, here is a list of some of the general terms used in French, German, Italian and Spanish patterns.

French Tatting Words

frivolité	tatting	*retournez de travail*	reverse work
navette	shuttle	*précédent*	previous
avec une navette	with one shuttle	*sautez*	miss
avec deux navettes	with two shuttles	*suivant*	following
anneau	ring	*tournez*	turn
arceau/chaine	chain	*laissez courir un peu de fil*	leave a space
noeud	(double) knot	*jusque au bout*	all round
demi-noeud	half knot	*nouez*	tie
picot	picot	*répétez*	repeat
fermez	close	*terminez*	finish
raccordez	join	*coupez*	cut
séparé	separated		

German Tatting Words

Schiffchenarbeit	tatting	*anschliessen*	join
Schiffchen	shuttle	*Arbeit wenden*	reverse work
Arbeitschiffchen	working shuttle	*vorhergehend*	previous
Schlingschiffchen	second shuttle	*Entfernung*	space
Ring	ring	*dazwischen*	between
Bogen	chain	*wiederholen*	repeat
Doppelknotten	double knot	*anschurzen*	tie
Pikot	picot	*abschneiden*	cut
zusammenziehen	close	*Faden*	thread

Italian Tatting Words

occhi	tatting	*chiudere*	close
il chiacchierino	tatting	*voltare il lavoro*	reverse work
lavoro a navetta	tatting	*ripetere*	repeat
navetta	shuttle	*come sopra*	as above
due navette	two shuttles	*attaccare*	attach, join
nodo	knot	*separato*	separated by
mezzi nodi	half stitches	*pippiolino*	picot
nodo Guiseppina	Josephine knot	*precedente*	previous
arca	chain	*giro precedente*	previous row
cerchio	ring	*filo*	thread
anello	ring		

Spanish Tatting Words

frivolité	tatting	*cerrar*	close
el encaje de lanzaderas	tatting	*pequeño*	small
anillo	ring	*grande*	large
pie	chain	*seguir*	continue
baguita	picot	*según*	according to
enganchar	join	*dar la vuelta*	reverse work

A Final Word

Now that you have learned to tat and have made all kinds of pretty things, the most important thing to do is to let people *know* about tatting.

Take it with you wherever you go, wear it on your clothing, wave your hankie with its tatted border everywhere! Don't let this lovely craft die. Teach someone to tat.

There are several tatting and lace organisations in Australia, England and the United States, all of which welcome new members. Some, such as the Ring of Tatters, are devoted to promoting and encouraging tatting. Others, such as the various Lace guilds, deal with all kinds of lace. Make enquiries—there is sure to be one somewhere near you.

Tatting is a great conversation-starter. Start tatting at a bus stop, in the train, in the doctor's waiting-room and before long all eyes will be on you. Someone will either ask you what you are doing or will tell you of her grandma, aunt, etc. who used to tat so fast you couldn't see how she did it! Try it and see! Even if you're not very good at tatting, to a non-tatter you will appear to be.

Finally, although I said there would be no collar pattern, due to many requests I have included one very easy one. It has only two rows, the first of which is worked with shuttle only for the length required, and as six rings are needed for each pattern repeat, with one ring between each repeat, be sure to count the number of rings you make for the first row.

The second row consists of an arch of seven rings and chains joined to the larger rings of the first row.

Both ends of the collar are the same so only one has been shown. Remember the last repeat will need only the six rings of the first row as you won't need the ring in between (see fig. 316).

Have fun and enjoyment with your tatting, and don't give up if you have trouble with that knot when you first start—it will come to you with a bit of practice, so keep at it.

Good tatting!

Rebecca Jones

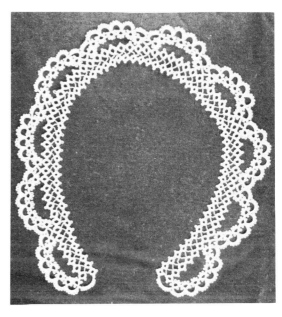

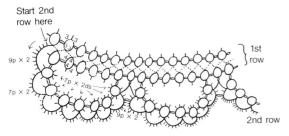

Fig. 316.   Simple collar made in 2 rows

An easy collar made in only two rows. The first row is made by shuttle only and the second has rings and chains.

Bibliography

Anon. *Tatting For Today.* 1980.
Anon. *Tatting.* 1981.
Anon. *Festive Tatting.* 1983.
 All published by D.M.C. Corporation, 107
 Trumball Street, Elizabeth, New Jersey 07206,
 U.S.A.

Anon. *Learn Tatting.*
Anon. *Tatting.*
Anon. *Time for Tatting.*
Anon. *Ten Tatting Designs.*
 All published by J & P Coats (UK) Ltd, 12
 Seedhill Road, Paisley, Scotland.

Attenborough, Bessie M. *The Craft of Tatting.*
 Published by Bell & Hyman Ltd, 37–39 Queen
 Elizabeth Street, London, SE1 2QB, England.
 1972

Auld, Rhoda. *Tatting.* Published by Van Nostrand
 Rheinhold Company, 135 West 50th Street,
 New York, New York 10020, U.S.A. 1974

De Dillmont, Therese. *The Complete Encyclopedia of
 Needlework.* Originally published by D.M.C.
 Library, Mulhouse, France, 1886. Present
 edition published by Running Press, 125 South
 Twenty Second Street, Philadelphia,
 Pennsylvania 19103, U.S.A.

Fujito, Sadako. *Tatting.* Published by Nihon Vogue
 Publishing Co. Ltd, 34 Ichigaya Honmuracho,
 Shinjuku-Ku, Tokyo 162, Japan. 1981. (I have
 only seen Japanese versions of this book, but all
 patterns are diagrams and easy to follow.)

Nicholls, Elgiva. *Tatting.* Now reprinted by Dover
 Publications Inc. (address below). *A New Look At
 Tatting* out of print now. *Tatting Techniques*
 published by Mills & Boon Ltd, 17–19 Foley
 Street, London W1A 1DR, England. 1976.

Sanders, Julia E. *Tatting Patterns.* Published by
 Dover Publications Inc., 180 Varick Street, New
 York, New York 10014, U.S.A. 1977 (Reprints
 of old patterns)

Waller, Irene. *Tatting.* Published by Studio Vista,
 Cassell, Collier & Macmillan Publishers Ltd, 35
 Red Lion Square, London WC1R 4SG,
 England. 1974

Weiss, Rita. *Tatting—Doilies & Edgings.* Published
 by Dover Publications Inc., 180 Varick Street,
 New York, New York 10014, U.S.A. 1980
 (Reprints of old patterns)

For information concerning the Jiffy Tatting Needle
write to: Edward A. Morin Company, P.O. Box
25376, Portland, Oregon 97225, USA.